T0250094

Beyond

KNOWLEDGE

Management

What Every Leader Should Know

Edited by Jay Liebowitz

CRC Press
Taylor & Francis Group
Boca Raton   London   New York

CRC Press is an imprint of the
Taylor & Francis Group, an **informa** business
AN AUERBACH BOOK

CRC Press
Taylor & Francis Group
6000 Broken Sound Parkway NW, Suite 300
Boca Raton, FL 33487-2742

International Standard Book Number: 978-1-4398-6250-6 (Hardback)

Library of Congress Cataloging-in-Publication Data

Beyond knowledge management : what every leader should know / editor, Jay Liebowitz.
     p. cm.
   Includes bibliographical references and index.
   ISBN 978-1-4398-6250-6 (hardcover : alk. paper)
     1. Leadership. 2. Executives. 3. Knowledge management. 4. Intellectual capital. 5. Social networks. 6. Technological innovations. I. Liebowitz, Jay, 1957-

HD57.7.B488 2012
658.4'092--dc23   2011037843

Visit the Taylor & Francis Web site at
http://www.taylorandfrancis.com

and the CRC Press Web site at
http://www.crcpress.com

To my wonderful family—Janet, Jason, Kenny, and Mazel

Contents

Preface

Senior leadership in organizations will continue to face challenging circumstances ahead. With recessionary times and global competition, senior executives have to do "much with less." Coupled with the external environmental issues, the aging workforce creates various knowledge retention and transfer concerns. Knowledge management is being used in many organizations to address ways to leverage knowledge better in order to increase innovation. Knowledge management is related to capitalizing on the intellectual assets in the organization. As such, the human capital in the organization is the competitive edge. In fact, Jim Goodnight, the CEO of SAS, once said that "95% of our assets at SAS walk out the front door every evening, and my job is to bring them back the next day."*

There are other important levers beyond knowledge management that senior executives can use in order to improve their strategic decision making and infuse vitality into their organizations. This is the focus of the book, namely, to make senior executives and managers better aware of emerging areas where they can derive value-added benefits in their organizations. It is easy to read, concise, and, it is hoped, meaningful.

Each of the chapters opens with an introduction to the chapter's topic and is followed by short case studies and vignettes from industry, government, and academia that support the chapter's focus. This helps to demonstrate further evidence on how organizations are applying these techniques for improved strategic decision making and operations.

I would like to thank the contributors of these cases who are leading individuals in their respective organizations. I would also like to express my gratitude to the Taylor & Francis publishing staff and my publishing editor, John Wyzalek, for producing such a timely and important book. A debt of gratitude goes to my University of Maryland University College colleagues, my students, and my professional friends outside the university. And certainly, without my wonderful family, and

---

* Leistner, F. (2010). *Mastering Organizational Knowledge Flow: How to Make Knowledge Sharing Work*. New York: John Wiley.

parents who taught me the value of education, this book would never have been possible.

Enjoy!

Jay Liebowitz, D.Sc.
Washington, D.C.

About the Editor

Dr. Jay Liebowitz is the Orkand Endowed Chair of Management and Technology in the Graduate School of Management & Technology at the University of Maryland University College (UMUC). He previously served as a professor in the Carey Business School at Johns Hopkins University. He is ranked as one of the top 10 knowledge management researchers/practitioners out of 11,000 worldwide, and was ranked number two worldwide in knowledge management strategy according to the January 2010 *Journal of Knowledge Management.* At Johns Hopkins University, he was the founding program director for the Graduate Certificate in Competitive Intelligence and the capstone director of the MS-Information and Telecommunications Systems for Business Program, where he engaged over 30 organizations in industry, government, and not-for-profits in capstone projects.

Prior to joining Hopkins, Dr. Liebowitz was the first knowledge management officer at NASA Goddard Space Flight Center. Before NASA, Dr. Liebowitz was the Robert W. Deutsch Distinguished Professor of Information Systems at the University of Maryland-Baltimore County, professor of management science at George Washington University, and chair of artificial intelligence at the U.S. Army War College.

Dr. Liebowitz is the founder and editor-in-chief of *Expert Systems with Applications: An International Journal* (published by Elsevier), which was ranked number one worldwide in the operations research/management science category according to the 2008 Thomson Impact Factors. He is a Fulbright Scholar, IEEE-USA Federal Communications Commission Executive Fellow, and Computer Educator of the Year (International Association for Computer Information Systems (IACIS)). In 2011, the annual Jay Liebowitz Outstanding Student Research Award was established through IACIS. He has published over 40 books and myriad journal articles on knowledge management, intelligent systems, and IT management. His most recent books are *Knowledge Retention: Strategies and Solutions* (Taylor & Francis, 2009), *Knowledge Management in Public Health* (Taylor & Francis, 2010), and *Knowledge Management and E-Learning* (Taylor & Francis, 2011). He has lectured and consulted worldwide. He can be reached at jliebowitz@umuc.edu.

Contributors

Joanne Andreadis
Centers for Disease Control and
Prevention
Atlanta, Georgia

Irena Bojanova
University of Maryland University
College
Adelphi, Maryland

Rhonda Chicone
Notify Technology Corporation
San José, California

Gregory Downing
U.S. Department of Health and
Human Services
Washington, D.C.

Luane Kohnke
R/GA
New York, New York

John Kools
Centers for Disease Control and
Prevention
Atlanta, Georgia

Denise Lee
PricewaterhouseCoopers
McLean, Virginia

Jay Liebowitz
University of Maryland University
College
Adelphi, Maryland

Scott MacLeod
R/GA
New York, New York

Sloane Menkes
PricewaterhouseCoopers
McLean, Virginia

Matthew North
Washington & Jefferson College
Washington, Pennsylvania

Sandeep Patnaik
Gallup & Robinson, Inc.
Pennington, New Jersey

Bob Payne
Northrop Grumman Corporation
El Segundo, California

Richard Schumaker
University of Maryland University
College
Adelphi, Maryland

Scott Shaffar
Northrop Grumman Corporation
El Segundo, California

Richard Staten
University of Maryland University
College
Adelphi, Maryland
and
Innovation Director
The Coca-Cola Company
Atlanta, Georgia

1

Gaining Competitive Advantage with Knowledge Management

Most CEOs will say that their organization's competitive advantage is "their people." That is, the human capital and associated intellectual capital assets are the main drivers for innovation and eventual competitive edge. If we make this assumption, then knowledge is at the root of this equation and thus, the ability to leverage knowledge effectively internally and externally should be a core competency for the organization. All this points to the area of "knowledge management" for competitive advantage.

Knowledge management (KM) as a field has emerged over the past 15 years, and tries to create value from the intellectual capital assets in the organization. Essentially, knowledge management focuses on how best to capture, share, apply, and leverage knowledge to ultimately gain competitive advantage. Organizations embark on their KM journeys for many reasons: to stimulate innovation, to enhance the adaptability and agility of the organization, to build the institutional memory of the organization before knowledge is lost, to strengthen the sense of community, and to improve the organization's internal and external effectiveness. Knowledge management also leads to improved decision making (du Plessis, 2005; Liebowitz, 2007–2010; Liebowitz et al., 2010; Liebowitz and Frank, 2011).

Typically, knowledge management involves three major components: people, process, and technology. The "people" side is how best to build and nurture a knowledge-sharing culture. The "process" component looks at embedding knowledge management processes within the daily work lives of the employees. Technology looks at creating a unified network for enabling knowledge sharing to take place. The typical 80–20 adage applies to knowledge management, where the people/process components are 80%, and technology is 20% of the pie.

Let's now turn to some examples of why knowledge management may be needed in an organization.

CASE 1: KNOWLEDGE TRANSFER NEEDED FOR NEWBIES

In the past two years, one organization hired about 150 new employees out of about 300 employees in the organization. At the same time, about 20 employees, including 3 key executives, were retiring within the coming year. There was a need for knowledge retention procedures of those who were retiring, but there was an even greater need for onboarding the new employees and bringing them up to speed to climb the learning curve quickly. A formal onboarding strategic initiative, as part of the organization's knowledge management strategy, was established to address this need. Cross-training, job rotation, job shadowing, lunch and learns, mentoring, regular training activities, and reverse mentoring (junior employees mentoring the more senior employees on technology and related issues) were being considered as part of the onboarding initiative.

As part of the overarching knowledge management initiative, the pilot programs under consideration were: a cross-office repository to store and access organization-produced documents and files; an enhanced organization-wide document management system; expertise locator system; knowledge retention SOP (standard operating procedures) for critical at-risk knowledge; lessons learned and after-action reviews; onboarding/new employee procedures; online communities of practice; recognition and rewards system for staff engaged in support of knowledge sharing, learning, and retention processes; and a searchable online multimedia knowledge repository.

A knowledge audit survey was completed by 40% of the organization's employees in order to better develop the knowledge management strategy for the organization. A Knowledge Management Working Group and associated subcommittees, with representation across all the divisions within the organization, were formed with a point person in charge of the knowledge management efforts in the organization. In two months, the organization accomplished the following:

- Created the active KM Working Group
- Established an awareness of KM at all levels within the organization—from senior management to staff positions—and showed how KM can

be integrated within the quality management and strategic planning processes within the organization

- Provided training to the organization on KM and how best to weave KM into its organizational fabric
- Developed and fielded the knowledge assessment survey used to formulate the KM strategy for the organization
- Established linkages with other groups outside the organization
- Populated online workspaces for collaboration
- Helped to jump-start a lessons learned process and associated lessons learned generic template for use within the organization
- Developed a draft Continuity Profile as an employee job hand-off guide for knowledge retention purposes
- Videotaped upcoming retirees as part of a knowledge preservation effort
- Helped in mentoring summer interns in the KM area

In the immediate future, the organization plans to analyze the knowledge assessment survey, develop a KM strategy with pilots/metrics/implementation plan, interview/videotape employees for knowledge preservation purposes, develop a knowledge retention SOP, actively pursue the onboarding initiative, and provide further training in the KM area.

CASE 2: KNOWLEDGE LOSS IS GREATER THAN KNOWLEDGE GAIN

The average age of the workforce in a global technical organization was 48. In completing a knowledge assessment survey, the average length of service was about 17 years. The employees' work experience with the organization was slightly skewed toward the upper end of years of experience. With this distribution and the fact that the Gen Yers have changing work patterns, this could put the organization in a precarious posture if knowledge retention and transfer procedures are not established, as critical "at-risk" knowledge could "walk out the door" as people retire.

To compensate for this possibility, the organization developed a KM strategy based on people, process, and technology. The people aspects looked at culture, networking, training and education, and retiree management.

The process aspects involved communities of practice to share ideas, lessons learned, and work practices, as well as establishing formal knowledge retention and transfer procedures and processes. Technology involved using the intranet and web-based technologies as an enabler for sharing knowledge.

Specific knowledge retention activities considered included (Liebowitz, 2010):

- Developing a knowledge map to be placed on the organization's intranet for preservation and expansion purposes can be a very useful aid. In specific, knowledge areas, this may include: FAQs (Frequently Asked Questions) → Answers → People/Department → Resources (Documents, SOPs, etc.). Concept mapping tools can be used to represent the relationships in a particular knowledge area.
- Continuity books, as used in the military, or job hand-off aids, as used in companies such as John Deere, can also be used to include what the typical job duties are, business processes, work flows, points of contact, and so on, to help one's successor quickly climb the learning curve.
- Desk-side reviews can be used where someone learns by exchanging templates, cheat sheets, and other job aids that may be in the desk drawers or on one's hard drive, instead of on the organization's shared drives.
- Mentoring programs, job shadowing, lunch and learn sessions, organizational narratives/storytelling, job rotation, wikis, blogs, expertise locator systems, online searchable multimedia asset management systems, lessons learned systems, do's and don't tutorials (webcast), and other knowledge retention (KR) approaches can be applied as appropriate.

DOES KM WORK?: KNOWLEDGE MANAGEMENT METRICS

In reviewing the literature, a number of organizations have approached KM metrics from the balanced scorecard, intellectual capital (e.g., Skandia's Intellectual Capital Navigator), activity-based costing, or some other approach borrowed from the accounting and human resources disciplines. Liebowitz (2008) shows case studies of organizations trying to measure knowledge management success. A few methodologies have examined ways to measure return on knowledge, such as Housel and Bell's (2001) Knowledge Value-Added (KVA) methodology. The KVA methodology can be applied to learning time or processes. For example, as applied to learning time, the steps are (Housel and Bell, 2001): (1) identify the core process and its subprocesses; (2) establish common units to measure learning time; (3) calculate learning time to execute each subprocess; (4) designate sampling time period long enough to capture a representative sample of the core process's final product/service output; (5) multiply the learning time for each subprocess by the number of times the subprocess executes during the sample period; (6) allocate revenue to subprocesses in proportion to the quantities generated by Step 5 and calculate costs for each subprocess; (7) calculate return on knowledge and interpret the results.

In reviewing over 50 articles on knowledge management metrics, KM metrics can be divided into system measures, output measures, and outcome measures. Susan Hanley and the Department of Navy-CIO highlight some of these measures in their publication, *Metrics for Knowledge Management Guide* (http://www.providersedge.com/docs/km_articles/Metrics_Guide_for_DON_KM_Initiatives.pdf). System measures deal with analytics associated with system-derived measures. Output measures relate to output associated with use of the system. Outcome measures, which are the most meaningful, deal with outcomes as associated with the strategic goals and mission of the organization that result from the use of the knowledge management application.

Based on the external review of KM metrics, Figure 1.1 shows the resulting concept map based on system, output, and outcome measures (Liebowitz, Clonmell, and Dardel, 2010). CMAPTools (http://cmap.ihmc.us/download/), from the University of West Florida, was the concept mapping software applied to generate these figures. Figure 1.1 shows an increasing number of KM metrics from system to output to outcome measures. As related to outcome measures, Liebowitz (2007) previously examined KM value-added benefits and found that most organizations use KM for five reasons: adaptability/agility, creativity, institutional memory building, organizational internal effectiveness, and organizational external effectiveness. The outcome measures, as shown in Figure 1.1, list the associated KM metrics in these categories.

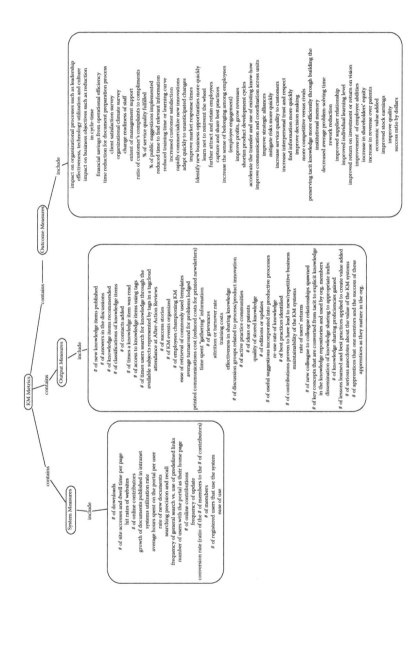

FIGURE 1.1

Concept map of KM metrics based on a review of the literature.

SPECIFIC KM METRICS RELATING TO VARIOUS KM APPROACHES

Various KM approaches are applied in organizations. The key approaches and associated outcome measures are shown below (Liebowitz, Clonmell, and Dardel, 2010).

Expertise Locator System (A Yellow Pages of Expertise in the Organization)

- Impact on business objectives such as reduction in cycle-time based on being able to locate the right person on a timely basis through the expertise locator system
- Financial savings from operational efficiency due to forming the right project team due to capitalizing on selected skills and availability resulting from using the expertise locator system
- Improved ratio of customer's complaints to compliments (i.e., increased customer satisfaction) due to knowing the right person to contact to address customer's concerns as a result of using the expertise locator system
- Percentage of service quality fulfilled
- Reduced time to find relevant information because the expertise locator system allows the quick identification of the right person who would have the information
- Reduced training time or learning curve
- Increase the sense of belonging and community among employees for improved employee engagement (can list hobbies, home town, etc. in the expertise locator system to develop and strengthen employee bonding)
- Improve decision making due to knowing the right person to address the questions from the expertise locator system
- New ideas generated by reaching out to others resulting from use of the expertise locator system
- Decrease average problem-solving time due to use of the expertise locator system
- Rework reduction
- Improve quality due to knowing the right person to contact through the expertise locator system

After-Action Reviews (AAR) (A Retrospective on What Worked Well, What Didn't Work, and How Can We Be Sure to Do It Correctly the Next Time)

- Accelerate the transfer and use of existing know-how through the AAR
- Reduced training time or learning curve
- Improve organizational decision making through capturing and sharing best practices/lessons learned
- Time reduction for document preparation process due to learning from others via the AAR
- Increased customer satisfaction due to learning from previous successes and failures and reacting expeditiously
- Improve quality of products through learning from others
- Improve continuous learning through the AAR process

Lessons Learned System (Best Practices Repository—Mixture of Outcome, System, and Output Measures)

- Ability to quickly capture LL (lessons learned) in the system
- Ability to improve performance and decision making through the embedded LL process
- Quality of the knowledge captured
- Amount of knowledge captured
- Ease of use in both incorporating LL into the process, as well as in accessing the LL
- Adaptability of the approach in terms of how generic is the methodology as applied to other domains
- Ease of archival and maintenance of the LL process
- Flexibility of the approach in terms of getting LL to the right user at the right time and in terms of searchability of the LL

Knowledge Capture Interviews

- Building the institutional memory so as not to reinvent the wheel
- Accelerate the transfer and use of existing know-how for increased learning
- Improvement of employee's abilities

Knowledge Video Nuggets

- Reduced rework through learning from others
- Increasing recognition for improved employee engagement
- Improve new hire retention rate through learning from others

Knowledge Cafés (Either Online Communities or In-Person Knowledge Sharing Sessions)

- Stronger sense of belonging and trust
- Innovations and creativity increased through knowledge sharing
- Improve decision-making time due to knowing others in your area (met through the knowledge cafés)

Wikis (Collaborative Editing Logs)

- Building the institutional memory for reducing individual/organizational learning time
- Work more efficiently by establishing project team wikis
- Reduce time to find appropriate information and knowledge

Blogs (Web Logs)

- Adapt quickly to unanticipated changes through real-time dialogue
- Improve communication and coordination across units
- Percentage of public suggestions implemented

SUMMARY

In the years ahead, knowledge management should be part of the fabric of the organization. Knowledge management can lead to innovation, and senior leaders will need to instill and nurture a knowledge-sharing culture in order to stimulate creativity for new products and services. In the following chapters, we take a look at other areas that go beyond knowledge management in which senior leaders must apply to gain a competitive advantage in their organizations.

REFERENCES

Du Plessis, M. (2005). Drivers of knowledge management in the corporate environment, *Int. J. Inf. Manage* 25,.

Housel, T. and Bell, A. (2001). *Measuring and Managing Knowledge*, New York: McGraw-Hill.

Liebowitz, J. (2007). *What They Didn't Tell You About Knowledge Management*, Lanham, MD: Scarecrow Press/Rowman & Littlefield.

Liebowitz, J. (2008). *Making Cents out of Knowledge Management*, Lanham, MD: Scarecrow Press/Rowman & Littlefield.

Liebowitz, J. (2009). *Knowledge Retention: Strategies and Solutions*, Boca Raton, FL: Taylor & Francis/CRC Press.

Liebowitz, J. (2010). Putting knowledge retention into practice, *IT Perf. Manage.*, September, http://www.ittoday.info/ITPerformanceImprovement/Articles/2010SeptLiebowitz.html

Liebowitz, J. and Frank, M. (Eds.) (2011). *Knowledge Management and E-Learning*, Boca Raton, FL: Taylor & Francis/CRC Press.

Liebowitz, J., Clonmell, M., and Dardel, A. (2010). *Working Notes on Knowledge Management Metrics*, Washington, DC: Plexus Scientific (for IRS Media and Publications).

Liebowitz, J., Schieber, R., and Andreadis, J. (Eds.) (2010). *Knowledge Management in Public Health*, Boca Raton, FL: Taylor & Francis/CRC Press.

2

Gaining Competitive Advantage with Strategic Intelligence

In today's organizations, we often hear the adage, "Work smarter, not harder." This is at the crux of this chapter in terms of applying strategic intelligence to help leaders make better decisions.

Strategic intelligence can be viewed as having three components (Liebowitz, 2006): business intelligence, competitive intelligence, and knowledge management. Business intelligence (BI) has an internal focus, competitive intelligence is more external, and knowledge management can be both internal and external, but is usually more internally directed. With business intelligence, the use of analytics (Davenport and Harris, 2007) and advanced information technologies is often applied to assist the decision maker. Competitive intelligence (CI) deals with establishing a program for collecting, analyzing, and managing external intelligence (such as competitors, environmental scans, etc.) to improve organizational decision-making. Knowledge management (KM), as we discussed in the last chapter, looks at leveraging knowledge both internally and externally, but typically has an inward focus on maximizing human capital and other intellectual assets in the organization. Together, the synergies among these three areas (BI, CI, and KM) can result in what the author calls "strategic intelligence" (SI).

BUSINESS INTELLIGENCE

Today's businesses must compete on analytics and improve their strategic intelligence in order to meet tomorrow's demands. Nash (2010) feels that companies must use business intelligence and analytics tools in order to figure out what is happening in their markets. According to Nash (2010), CUNA Mutual has mined its customer data to determine which of its products are selling, why, and to whom. Sixty-five percent of 335 IT leaders indicated that business intelligence and analytics have created a business process change in the last year (Nash, 2010). David White with the Aberdeen Group studied 159 organizations that actively use predictive analytics and determined that the best-in-class companies retain 93% percent of their customers, compared to laggards who retain just 66% (Nash, 2010). Analytics tools are being integrated with customer-relationship management systems to create better processes for customer engagement.

Numerous companies are deriving great benefits from the use of analytics. Ingersoll Rand discovered the use of some incorrect data about supplier lead times through analytics. Welch's cut 12–15% from its $50 million in annual transportation costs based on its use of analytics (Nash, 2010). Princess Cruises uses analytics to better target customer promotions (Harris, 2010). Harrah's uses a service profit chain model to improve customer loyalty and target key decision areas (Harris, 2010).

In Davenport and Jarvenpaa's (2008) report on "Strategic Use of Analytics in Government," even the federal government is applying analytics to meet their goals. Specifically, the domains of healthcare, logistics, revenue management, and intelligence are using analytics to improve their decision-making processes. The Veterans Health Administration, for example, is a leading healthcare provider in the use of evidence-based medicine (Davenport and Jarvenpaa, 2008). Although analytics are being used in the government in selected areas, Davenport and Jarvenpaa (2008) point out that there needs to be a generation of analytical "leadership" in order to apply these techniques in strategic ways.

In spite of the advantages to using analytics, there are still numerous organizations that have not been applying analytics for good decision making. According to the 2010 Gartner-FERF Technology Issues for Financial Executives Survey, financial executives believe that in spite of investments that have been made in technology, their organization does not have the information it needs to analyze its operation and drive financial performance (Rohrecker, 2010). The collection, analysis, and management of this business information should be part of the business and competitive intelligence operations of the organization. Organizations must align their business intelligence and operational systems strategies (Saporito, 2010). According to Saporito (2010), as business intelligence is pushed out operationally onto employee desktops and to business partners, an increasing need exists for self-service reporting tools, text analytics, data exploration, predictive modeling, and advanced analytics.

As best explained by Davenport, Harris, and Morison (2010), organizations should look at the following conditions for applying analytics:

- Complex decisions with many variables and steps
- Simple decisions in which consistency is either desirable or required by law
- Places where you need to optimize the process or activity as a whole
- Decisions in which you need to understand connections, correlations, and their significance
- Places where you need better forecasts and anticipation

COMPETITIVE INTELLIGENCE

Business intelligence has primarily an internal focus, whereas competitive intelligence is more externally oriented. Both types of intelligence, along with knowledge management, contribute to the organization's overall strategic intelligence.

According to Guidebook, Inc. (2010), many Fortune 500 companies have entire departments devoted to competitive intelligence. In fact, we can also look more broadly in terms of what Thomas Malone from MIT's Center for Collective Intelligence is coining "collective intelligence." He is looking at using new technologies to amplify human intelligence (MIT, 2010). But certainly organizations must apply business intelligence techniques to determine market intelligence better. Today, market intelligence is more socially engaged, as Hedin (2010) points out. Cisco Systems bought 300 iPods for its senior managers to plug into podcasts and videocasts on the latest market developments and analyses that are produced by its in-house intelligence team (Hedin, 2010). Blog-rating websites, crowd forecasting, wikis, corporate intelligence portals integrated with customer relationship management systems, and other social media will continue to play a role for data- and text-mining applications.

When we look at an organization, we can view it in terms of four different types of intellectual capital. Human capital is the employee's brainpower and experience, which often provides the competitive edge for the organization. Structural capital is the knowledge that you can't easily bring home with you from the office, such as intellectual property rights. Social, relationship, or customer capital is what you learn from your customers. Last, competitor capital is what you learn from your competition. This latter capital is where competitive intelligence plays a key role.

Rothberg and Erickson (2005) define competitive intelligence as finding what you need by using what you know. In looking at competitive intelligence, it typically involves the collection, analysis, and management processes involved in gathering, analyzing, and managing competitive intelligence. The majority of the effort seems to be put in the collection phase, much to the chagrin of the organization as not enough effort is typically put in the analysis phase. Techniques such as simulations or war gaming, scenario-building, environmental scanning, forward-looking analysis, early warning and risk management, SWOT (strengths-weaknesses-opportunities-threats) analysis, value chain analysis, patent analysis, competitive hypothesis analysis, defense and aggressive reputation analysis, blind spot analysis, management profiling, and other analytical approaches and tools should be applied, as appropriate, during the competitive intelligence process. Creative thinking must also be used to complement these analytical approaches. And, analysis is not a substitute for synthesis (Fiora, 2005). Competitive intelligence professionals must produce a true actionable analysis that is forward-looking and decision-relevant (Fiora, 2005).

A CASE STUDY: USING DATA MINING TO DETECT VULNERABLE "AT RISK" STUDENTS FOR IMPROVING RETENTION AND COMPLETION RATES

Data mining is a business intelligence technique that can be used to uncover hidden relationships and patterns in large masses of data. Many organizations, especially in retail, telecommunications, marketing, and the like, are using data-mining techniques to improve organizational decision making in terms of how best to attract and retain customers, how to reduce customer churn, what complementary sets of products might interest a customer, and other similar types of decisions. Data mining uses supervised or unsupervised learning in order to identify patterns, trends, and anomalies. KDNuggets.com (www.kdnuggets.com) is a website geared to the data mining community.

Applying data mining in education is a growing field. The November 10, 2010 blog entry on "Massive Scale Data Mining for Education" (http://cacm.acm.org/blogs/blog-cacm/101489-massive-scale-data-mining-for-education/fulltext) talks about the tremendous opportunities to use data mining for educational purposes, especially with the increased use of online learning. In this vein, the University of Maryland University College (UMUC) received a large grant in October 2010 by the Kresge Foundation to use data-mining techniques aimed at improving retention and completion rates of disadvantaged adult students in Maryland. As most of the courses at UMUC are taught through e-learning, via the UMUC-developed WebTycho e-learning platform, almost all of the transactions are captured, providing a wealth of data to mine and identify those students who may potentially have difficulty during the early parts of their university programs. Once found, those students can receive the necessary support services to help them achieve success in getting through the program for graduation.

IBM Modeler (formerly SPSS Clementine) is the data mining tool that will likely be applied on this project. According to the October 26, 2010 UMUC Press Release (http://www.umuc.edu/umucmedia/press/news328.shtml), the following was stated:

> University of Maryland University College (UMUC) announced today that it has been awarded a $1.2 million grant from The Kresge Foundation to develop—in partnership with Prince George's Community College (PGCC) and Montgomery College (MC)—predictive models and success interventions designed to help close the achievement gap for underserved adult students in Maryland. The project aims to improve student retention and completion rates through data mining techniques, and will be conducted over a three-year period.
>
> "UMUC is committed to providing flexible, affordable, high-quality programs for our students, most of whom work full-time or serve in the military while juggling family responsibilities," said UMUC President Susan C. Aldridge. "This generous grant from The Kresge Foundation will allow us to explore the gap in student success, retention and graduation rates. It will help us and our community college partners to identify the factors that hinder some students from reaching their education goals and allow us to develop better strategies for intervening proactively on their behalf."
>
> Research from the Georgetown University Center on Education and the Workforce indicates that by 2018, more than 68 percent of all jobs will require some post-secondary education—an increase of 40 percent from current needs. The grant project will help meet this increased need

by focusing on working adults who matriculate at a community college, and then pursue a bachelor's degree. Through this project, UMUC and its community college partners will implement a three-staged process that includes extracting and analyzing student data from each school, identifying strategies of successful and unsuccessful students to create evidence-based strategies and advising approaches to maximize student success, and developing and disseminating the results.

The grant will also enable UMUC and its partners to develop an integrated database system to build predictive models designed to increase rates of continuous enrollment and eventual graduation. Ultimately, the project will yield a replicable process based on data-driven practices that will lead to increases in student persistence and graduation rates.

This project is an example of how organizations can apply business intelligence techniques, specifically data-mining analytics, in order to improve decision making. In this example, the university is concerned about its core businesses—that is, student retention and completion—and through data-mining techniques, the hope is that these methods will aid in improving student persistence and graduation rates.

The next section discusses how analytics and data visualization play a key role in helping organizations derive greater value.

Real-Time Data, Real-Time Decisions

Luane Kohnke and Scott MacLeod
R/GA

INTRODUCTION

In the past, marketers relied on focus groups, ethnographic studies, brainstorming, and other controlled laboratory environments to understand customers: what they need, what makes them tick, and what drives their decisions. Today consumers are engaged in real-time with the brand in social settings, on websites, and in digital media, especially search. Although people's behaviors have not dramatically changed—we still gossip, rant, refer, shop, and buy—these behaviors are now more frequently occurring in digital channels. As a result, the measurable nature of digital media has provided us with much more sophisticated ways of constantly tracking and analyzing what people say, feel, and do online. We as marketers are hooked up to a vast and continuous data stream that can tell us *exactly* what consumers need and how they are behaving right now.

Learning can be continuous and in real-time. Marketing has become equal parts outbound communication and inbound listening, learning, managing, and responding to the data stream. As such, brands are no longer static icons, but dynamic systems, where there is a value exchange between the brand and its members, a set of norms that define brand behavior, and a common set of values that flow through the system. Marketing has entered a new era of learning, shaped by a continuous stream of customer data (Charnock, 2010). As a result, data mining and data visualization are emerging as robust analytics approaches to help us synthesize and present insights in new and more meaningful ways.

So, what exactly is this data stream and how does it (or should it) shape the relationships we have with our customers in a digital space? Who is using it to their benefit and how has it defined their business strategies?

THE NEW REALITY

All research begins with a business problem:

- I need to make more money.
- I need to sell more widgets.
- My customers are leaving me.
- I need younger people to like my product.

We take these business problems and shape our research and insight questions accordingly. We bring people into laboratory-style focus groups or quantitative research studies and ask them: "Why do you like this widget?" "What would make you buy more of it?" or "Do you like this different shape of widget?"

The problem is that this has very little to do with what the customer *really* wants and how he or she behaves in the real world. Even the broadest and most generic consumer surveys are still geared toward product consumption. We might ask questions about lifestyle and interests, but these are carefully crafted around a set of markets and potential products. Never do we simply say, "So tell me what's going on with you at the moment."

But then, along came digital and the opportunity to get out of the lab and into the real world. Instead of thinking about what we want and what the business is trying to achieve, we can simply listen, watch, and learn from the real behavior of real consumers. If we are constantly tuned into consumers digitally then we become active observers of real behavior and real trends. We do not need to ask people too much about what motivated them or how they will use our product because most of the information we need is right there in front of us. But we do need to mine the data for insights and ideas.

This has moved our approach from "asking" to "observation." Because we are often not asking direct questions of consumers the same way a survey would, we instead have to look for certain signals in the data to indicate what the answers are. This observation requires structured approaches to mining the vast array of data. Sometimes we need to posit hypotheses of why consumers are behaving in a certain way, and sometimes we need to use analytical approaches to categorize and cluster the behavior before we begin looking for answers.

NEW SOURCES CREATE NEW LISTENING POSTS

In the same way that call center data provide a "listening post" for product and service failures, web analytics, social media platforms, and search engine data can displace research surveys, focus groups, and panels. These data sources can be tapped to give a broad and deep view of real-time consumer behavior and opinions.

Web analytics (both on our own sites and in the competitive environment) allow the observation of every customer as he walks through our "store," and note everything that he touches and considers, what he reads or reviews, where he comes from, and where he goes next.

Social media platforms give us insight into why consumers love (or hate) our products and how that is reflected back on our brand. As marketers we no longer are forced to pursue consumers to get opinions. Today, we can eavesdrop on thousands, if not millions, of real consumers having a real unfiltered conversation about us. As brands, we can respond back either in the moment of the conversation or act outside the conversation to change our products and our brand. In many ways social media enable the virtual circle of planning, executing, evaluating, and responding to be realized in real-time.

Search engines are another unimaginably vast and detailed "database of human behavior" where we can literally track what the

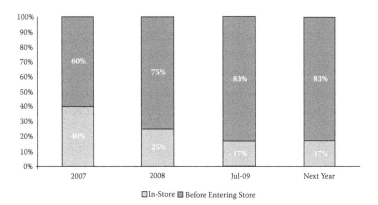

FIGURE 2.1
IRI shopper behavior 2009.

collective human consciousness is looking for next. But how exactly is this changing the game? How can we use this immense and exciting opportunity to our advantage? In July 2011, Google published a marketing book that showed that over 80% of shoppers make up their minds about which product to buy before they ever enter a store. For example, fast food customers go online to research the caloric value of their lunch options in advance of going to the fast food outlet and placing an order. Women research a recipe online before going to the grocery store and buying only what is needed for the recipe. This fact points to the importance of harnessing search to guide consumer preference and purchase intent early in the process of discovery. Understanding search behavior is necessary to make real-time marketing decisions. Figure 2.1 shows shopper behavior in 2009.

A BALANCE OF "TOP-DOWN" AND BOTTOM-UP" ANALYSIS IS REQUIRED

Top-down means we know what we are looking for—how a certain segment purchases electronics online or what people think about organic coffee—and using focused analysis to find it. The key to this is a strong question or hypothesis. We categorize data into relevant groupings and look for support to confirm (or deny) our theory.

For example, if we were looking to understand what consumers thought about Brand A's electronics products, we would start with a list of product names, product types, and other key words or phrases that clearly reflect our knowledge of the topic in a concise manner. Since the business value of the analysis is directly related to the depth of topic knowledge, generating the right key word framework is essential. Furthermore, refining the framework is necessary, making most top-down analyses iterative. The broader the subject matter, such as "tell me what people are saying about Brand X," the more iterations are likely. The narrower the subject, "tell me about what people are saying about toothbrushes," the simpler it will be to refine the results.

In mining social media conversations, we would utilize the following process:

- Identify keywords by: reading comments/posts, using search results to understand consumer language, or reviewing survey data on the topic
- Refine the conversation framework and keyword filters

Bottom-up analysis means we do not know what we are looking for—at least at first. By clustering data using statistical methods, we can uncover previously unobserved trends. The key here is statistical analysis and disciplined categorization Analysis and data exploration can uncover emerging trends and help us to see relationships in data that were previously unknown. This type of observation through data mining provides valuable insights that are instructional in evaluating future hypotheses. Bottom-up data mining and exploration underscores the untapped power of massive data sets found in social media, web analytics, and search data.

For example, a social media bottom-up analysis would use text mining, clustering, and proximity linguistic analysis to categorize comments. Once categories were established, additional layers of detail could be developed, such as

- Volume and sentiment by category
- Conversation content layers within a category
- Seasonal trends (volume, sentiment and content)
- Source of content (blogs, twitter, Facebook, etc.)
- Cross-category themes, such as lowest price, good value, etc.

Bottom-up social media analysis could provide useful benchmarks for category volume and sentiment, and could aid period-over-period analysis. Figure 2.2 shows a social media analytics framework.

Tactical	Strategic
Results	
Campaign Impact •Alerts •Reporting	Business and Brand Impact •Channel Impact •Social Media "Return"
Marketing Insights •Brand Sentiment •Conversation Analysis •Informed Feedback	Audience Dimensions •Influentials •Advocates
	Trend Analysis •Among Consumers •Across Channels
Insights	

FIGURE 2.2
Social media analytics framework.

RESPONDING IN REAL-TIME

If information, insight, and data are the foundations and bedrock of marketing strategy, then harnessing the power of real-time information will cause a seismic shift in the way we act on information. The shift toward real-time data and continuous knowledge of customer behavior gives us an opportunity to see the world in a different way and to change what we do. Organizations have already started to mine the continuous streams of web, social, and search data with some interesting results. But what lies ahead? We see the following three critical focus areas emerging for organizations that want to tap into and master the data stream.

DATA VISUALIZATION: MAKING SENSE OF THE DATA STREAM

Data visualization is the "new black" of analytics' disciplines (Singer, 2011; Jones-Dilworth, 2010). What is it? It is using graphical displays to create a picture with data that easily and concisely conveys a story. The best data visualizations are interactive, allowing the user to drill down or zoom out of the data. Often time or geography is the unifying variable that creates the compelling insights. Massive amounts of data not only need data mining to organize them into interesting facts, but also need data visualization to tell a compelling story.

One example of this is UPS, whose transportation engineers have adopted data visualization as a way to identify unrealized efficiencies in their transportation networks. By visualizing these data using Tableau, (tableausoftware.com) a leading business analytics company,

UPS was able to uncover previously unseen trends in network utilization and optimize its resources accordingly. These efforts yielded UPS $2.5M in efficiencies and a significant return on their analytics investment (http://www.tableausoftware.com/support/knowledge-base/troubleshooting-server-backup-and-restores).

CONTINUOUS OPTIMIZATION: REACTING TO THE DATA STREAM

Algorithms that utilize real-time data streams have enabled marketers such as Amazon to merchandise their sites and market to consumers based on the ever-changing interests of their customers and passers-by. Amazon's strategy has been firmly rooted in continuous change and evolution. Its business moves forward on a continuous wave of search engine optimization, behavioral targeting, recommendations algorithms, and on-site optimization driven by web analytics. For example, in January 2011 Amazon announced that it will publish 16 books in its AmazonEncore imprint and eight books in its AmazonCrossing imprint. Both imprints used Amazon's extensive sales data and customer reviews to help inform publishing decisions. "Our team of editors uses this data as a starting point to identify strong candidates, then applies their judgment to narrow the list and reach out to the authors," Jeff Belle, VP, Amazon.com Books, told LJ. "We're fortunate to have access to both a lot of sales information, as well as an editorial team made up of book lovers," he said. Amazon is a terrific example of using real-time, continuous data to drive change through actionable insights (Kelley, 2011).

DEMOCRATIZING DATA: SHARING THE DATA STREAM

As data become more available, and both legible (through visualization) and actionable (through optimization), they have the power to influence decisions across an entire company, beyond those the original decision makers targeted or anticipated. Organizations are taking data and making it accessible in an interactive, filterable, and visual format, so that many users across their company are able to explore and select the perspectives that they need to answer questions beyond the original intent of the data. Data are no longer confined to a fixed view by region, category, product, or channel. Data are now more malleable, filterable, and ultimately valuable to an organization (Varian, 2008).

One U.S. retailer is now sharing and leveraging real-time social media conversations to drive decisions across its organization. Once confined to corporate marketing audiences, these data are now providing local store operators with insights about what departments are popular and how customers perceive prices and quality. These local store operators now have a real-time window into their specific customers' needs and wants. They are able to adjust promotions, pricing, selection, and staffing to react to this new knowledge.

Not only have local store operators changed store merchandising and featured items, but the company has also created more socially active programs by asking shoppers to submit their own product stories and sharing the best ones within the store. Local store operators are able to act on insights in a just a few days and see the results immediately in store traffic patterns and purchase activity.

SUMMARY

As marketers, we no longer live in a world where we have to second-guess our customers. The vast wealth of continuous data offered to us by the adoption of digital technology is one of the greatest opportunities we have ever had. The most important question we must ask ourselves as marketers is how do we use this vast amount of data to our advantage. What tools, techniques, and processes are available to organize the raw data, find insights, and drive decision making? How can we evolve our organizations to thrive in a world where learning is continuous and the brand changes daily? How can we use the data stream to take our companies to new places and not become overwhelmed by the rush of information?

FINAL THOUGHT

Organizations should apply business and competitive intelligence in order to maximize their strategic intelligence. Senior leadership must champion the use of these techniques in order to help them and their management teams make improved decisions in the future. Today's organizations should be engaged with these approaches, without which, social Darwinism (i.e., survival of the fittest) will surely result, weeding out the weaker firms in favor of the stronger ones.

REFERENCES

Charnock, W., with J. Longden (2010). Real-time CRM: Ride the Perpetual Data Stream, *Admap*, December 2010, p 21-23.

Davenport, T. and Harris, J. (2007). *Competing on Analytics: The New Science of Winning*, Cambridge, MA: Harvard Business Press.

Davenport, T. and Jarvenpaa, S. (2008). *Strategic Use of Analytics in Government*, Washington, DC: IBM Center for the Business of Government.

Davenport, T., Harris, J., and Morison, R. (2010). *Analytics at Work: Smarter Decisions, Better Results*, Cambridge, MA: Harvard Business School.

Fiora, B. (2005). The 7 Deadly Sins of CI, *Strategic and Competitive Intelligence Professionals Conference*, Alexandria, VA, April, www.scip.org.

Guidebook, Inc. (2010). How to keep tabs on the competition, 2: 1, April.

Harris, J. (2010). Energize the business with analytics, *Computer Weekly*, March 9–15.

Hedin, H. (2010). Market intelligence is now more socially engaged. *Information Today*, April.

Jones-Dilworth, J. (2010). 5 Predictions for Online Data in 2011, *Mashable*, December 20.

Kelley, M. (2011). Amazon Continues Its Push into Publishing, *Library Journal.com*, February 2.

Lecinski, J. (2011). *Winning the Zero Moment of Truth*, Google Inc.

Liebowitz, J. (2006). *Strategic Intelligence: Business Intelligence, Competitive Intelligence, and Knowledge Management*, Boca Raton, FL: Taylor & Francis/CRC Press.

MIT (2010). Collective brainpower, IEEE *Spectrum*, Summer.

Nash, K. (2010). Analyzing the future: When business intelligence is used to inform business process changes, companies find new ways to save money and connect more closely with customers, *CIO Magazine*, 23: 14, July 1.

Rohrecker, K. (2010). Combine data and acumen to fill information gaps, *Financial Executive*, May, www.financialexecutives.org.

Rothberg, H. and S. Erickson (2005). *From Knowledge to Intelligence: Creating Competitive Advantage in the Next Economy*, Elsevier/Buttersworth-Heinemann, Burlington, MA.

Saporito, P. (2010). Get smart, *Best's Review*, May.

Singer, N. (2011). When Data Struts Its Stuff, *The New York Times*, April 2.

Varian, H. (2008). The Democratization of Data, *Official Google Blog*, September 21.

3

Gaining Competitive Advantage with Globalization

As Thomas Friedman echoes in his books, "the world is flat." Many organizations have 24/7 operations that span the world, such as in the case of globally distributed software teams. Outsourcing, off-shoring, and other techniques are being applied so organizations can, it is hoped, remain competitive in the global marketplace. In the United States we are seeing increasing competition from India, China, Brazil, and other international players. With intellectual capital being high in those countries and labor costs being relatively low, U.S. competition for products and services is at a difficult crossroads. Global partnerships need to be created to ensure competitive pricing, and the educational systems worldwide must be able to adjust to the new educational demands in the global marketplace.

For example, let's take a look at the information technology (IT) industry in terms of emerging needs for talent in the coming years. According to Hoffmann (2010), the Bureau of Labor Statistics (BLS) projects that computing will be one of the fastest growing job markets through 2018 in the United States. Of the new jobs created, 27% will be in software engineering, 21% in computing networking, and 10% in systems analysis. According to the BLS, software engineering alone is expected to add nearly 300,000 jobs in the United States in the next eight years (Hoffmann, 2010). The challenge, however, is that we are not graduating enough majors in computer science and related fields, even though the number of undergraduate computer science majors in the United States has slightly increased recently (however, the number of U.S. PhDs in computer science has dropped). According to the BLS, there will be more than twice as many new computing jobs per year in the next eight years than the current level of 50,000 computing graduates will be able to fill (Hoffmann, 2010).

Is this trend typical of just the United States? The answer is, "Not really." Looking internationally, enrollment in computer science programs in the United Kingdom has dropped by nearly 60% over the past eight years (Hoffmann, 2010). In China, the number of university undergraduates has increased dramatically during the past 10 years; however, recent computer science graduates in China are also struggling with a demanding job market (Hoffmann, 2010). In India, the IT industry is rebounding after the global downturn and the IT services sector in India grew 16.5% in 2009 (Hoffmann, 2010). However, a key concern in India is the lack of educators to teach the next generation of software engineers, a shortage of up to 70,000 teachers (Hoffmann, 2010).

Having the right combination of talent and commercial goods is a global competitive balance that organizations must endure. Developing and maintaining relationships is key for future organizational success, especially in this global competitive marketplace.

GLOCALIZATION

Over the years, the term "glocalization" has been used to combine "globalization" and "localization." The idea here is that products and services that are marketed and sold abroad should be tailored to the local culture. When careful attention to the locale is not given sufficient focus, problems will invariably ensue. For example, when EuroDisney first opened in France, many of the customs, rules, and procedures that worked at Disneyland in the United States were imposed on the French, which quickly proved to be disastrous. When customs were realigned, Disneyland Paris became a happier place to work.

According to Shopperculture.com, the next growth phase for big retailers is about segmentation and localization: multiple formats targeting specific customers, markets, and end-use needs (http://www.shopperculture.com/shopper_culture/glocalization/). And now through social networking, search, and related technologies, multinational companies have a wealth of data to better target their wares to the local customer. In a sense, the world has become smaller through the modern miracles of bits and bytes. Many help desk centers are in India and Asia, and when a U.S. customer calls about a problem, he or she typically reaches one of these help desk centers to troubleshoot the problem. However, the troubleshooter (with the modified American accent and name) has at his fingertips the colloquialisms to use programmed into the computer so it appears that you are reaching someone in the United States (again at a local level), even though you are reaching someone many thousands of miles away. Some companies, such as Rural Outsourcing Inc. in Atlanta, are setting up on-shoring operations in small towns in the United States with low-cost workers laid off from the recession to compete against off-shoring services (spidi2.iimb. ernet.in/~networth/2010801.pdf).

DEVELOPING AN INTERNATIONAL STRATEGY

Today's organizations must decide how best to globalize their operations, if at all. For example, many large technology-based corporations have research centers based not only in their region of the world (say, Asia, for example), but also have research centers elsewhere in Europe and in the United States. Similarly, many corporations have manufacturing plants in different parts of the world to capitalize on the local markets, as well as on lower labor and material costs. Unions, laws and regulations, politics, an educated workforce, and many other considerations also play a major role in developing a global strategy.

Stephen Davis with CXO Advisory Group highlights 10 common exporter mistakes in developing an international market strategy (http://www.slideshare.net/stephendaviscxo/developing-your-international-market-strategy):

1. Insufficient commitment by management
2. Going global before the domestic market is fully established
3. Failing to develop a full go-to-market plan
4. Using wrong criteria for selecting markets to enter
5. Trying to enter too many new markets at one time
6. Failing to establish a budget up front
7. Not localizing the product
8. Running afoul of U.S. export regulations
9. Selecting the wrong distribution channel
10. Ignoring international markets when the U.S. market is doing well

Kumar, Deivasigamani, and Omer (2010) also point out that globalization is transforming the working world where the migration of jobs is part of a low-cost high-performance strategy that can lead to competitive advantage. Kumar et al. (2010) indicate that Forrester Research estimates that 3.3 million jobs could be lost to off-shoring by 2015, whereby 500,000 knowledge-based jobs could shift from the United States to India, China, or Russia. The authors point out that off-shoring can create a competitive advantage by gaining flexibility, focusing on core competency, company survival, and productivity. However, disadvantages may ensue, namely improper management, hidden costs, and security/intellectual property risks (Kumar et al., 2010).

Much has been written about outsourcing, especially from an information technology perspective. Lee and Kim (1999) researched the effect of partnership quality on IT outsourcing. In examining 74 outsourcing relationships between 36 service receivers and 54 service providers, partnership quality was found to be positively influenced by factors such as participation, communication, information sharing, and top management support, and negatively affected by age of relationship and mutual dependency (Lee and Kim, 1999). Ten years later, Overby (2009) stated that the IT outsourcing market had reached a major tipping point whereby traditional deals would continue to decrease during the next several years as new utility and cloud service offerings proliferate. And in 2011, according to Entrepreneur Buddy (2010), there will be a high demand for global delivery capabilities, growing demand for mobile software development, increased use of agile software development, greater use of transformational outsourcing whereby an outsourcer will take over the entire product or application development process (and possibly manage the entire business function), and expanded use of public and private clouds. The IT, financial, automotive, media, telecom, and other industries will continue to look toward using outsourcing to their benefit.

OUTSOURCING ISSUES RELATED TO CURRENCY FLUCTUATIONS

According to the PricewaterhouseCoopers 13th Annual Global CEO Survey, approximately 90% of companies cut costs in 2009 (McKenzie and Henderson, 2010). "Many companies put outsourcing plans on hold and renegotiated existing contracts with outsourcing providers at lower prices, in exchange for contract extensions and other trade-offs, such as adjustments to service levels" (McKenzie and Henderson, 2010). In the near term, we will see increased contract renegotiations mostly caused by the recession and more use of outsourcing contract clauses to adjust to currency fluctuations. In addition, outsourcing contracts are also trending toward fewer service levels with more flexibility (McKenzie and Henderson, 2010).

Companies are looking closely at the euro crisis. For example, Audi suspended plans to build a U.S.-specific model in the States as the value of the euro has fallen off against the dollar, making this option less attractive (Bowman, 2010). The following are the major off-shoring locations, according to Diaz (2009):

- *India:* The most popular location for U.K. companies to off-shore their back-office operations.
- *China:* Many outsourcing providers have expanded into this market and U.S. companies, such as Avaya, have transitioned operations here.
- *Philippines:* Another popular location with U.S. companies.
- *Ukraine:* A new emerging market, the Ukraine offers a range of skills from the expected low-end processing through to higher-end services such as knowledge process outsourcing (KPO), which is not so typical of this type of location.
- *Poland*: A popular near-shore location for some time with the likes of several companies, such as UBS and Shell, having operations here.
- *Romania*: A near-shore location with a high-quality skilled and multilingual labor pool, low property costs, and growing infrastructure has led companies such as Betfair, to have their operations here.
- *Hungary*: Like Romania, Hungary is also known for its high-quality skilled labor and low costs with the likes of companies such as Diageo and Siemens running operations here.
- *Czech Republic*: A location with high-quality skilled labor and a focus on improving infrastructure and business environment with companies such as DSG International running operations here.

Certainly, with the foreign currency fluctuations throughout the world, each of these popular off-shoring locations will feel some impact in the years ahead.

We now turn to a specific case study by Richard Staten describing some of the strategic globalization and innovation efforts at The Coca-Cola Company in order to gain a competitive advantage.

Harnessing Globalization: The Case of Innovation at The Coca-Cola Company*

Richard C. Staten
University of Maryland University College
(Innovation Director, The Coca-Cola Company)

INTRODUCTION

This case considers the strategic actions of The Coca-Cola Company to continue its record of growth across global beverage markets, successfully rising to its position as the world's largest beverage company, frequently recognized for its consumer marketing and distribution strategies that have created long-standing competitive advantages. Although these are certainly true of The Coca-Cola Company's rise, the company continues to capture sustainable growth and new competitive advantages through additional new strategies relevant to a changing world with a specific focus on rising economies such as Brazil, Russia, India, and China in addition to its longstanding markets. Here in this case, we consider how establishing innovation-enabled strategies, a network of global knowledge centers, a common innovation process, and reapplications of promising innovations across the world have positioned The Coca-Cola Company to harness globalization for growth.

Few organizations have the track record of The Coca-Cola Company when it comes to successful and sustained expansion beyond their home market. The Coca-Cola Company has evolved from origins of a single product introduced in a pharmacy in the Deep South during the post-Reconstruction Era of the United States into a well-respected corporate citizen selling products across channels in the global marketplace. Some excellent examples of this record are The Coca-Cola Company's early partnership as a sponsor of the Olympic Games as well as their strategy of global distribution to supply deployed American servicemen during the Second World War. These are well-known, foundational strategic moves that helped cement The Coca-Cola Company's position in world markets that eventually led them to rise to the world's largest beverage company.

In the first example, The Coca-Cola Company established a connection between their flagship brand and the most globally inclusive

---

* Coca-Cola®, Coca-Cola Zero®, Diet Coke®, Fanta®, Minute Maid®, and Sprite® are registered trademarks of The Coca-Cola Company.

sporting championship events (Our Partnership History, 2008). The Olympic Games are an international event and as such a sports marketing platform with global reach to consumers. This provides an ability to reach worldwide audiences with a message that Coca-Cola is a global brand, not just an export from the United States. The other way that The Coca-Cola Company delivered on this aspect was that their product is globally produced at local bottling facilities. This distribution scale was propelled by a strategy driven by then-Chairman and CEO Robert W. Woodruff of a guarantee for global supply to U.S. servicemen during the Second World War (The Chronicle of Coca-Cola, 2011). The strategy provided for the establishment of over 60 new bottling operations in countries across Europe, Africa, and Asia. After the hostilities ended and the U.S. troops returned home, these operations were not dismantled but rather were kept in place for civilian populations who had adopted Coca-Cola as their soft drink of choice during the war. These two examples have been the subject of many authors who have studied the history of The Coca-Cola Company, however, they are both strategies introduced over six decades ago.

Turning now to the most recent decade, a new imperative for innovation success has arisen out of The Coca-Cola Company's strategies, beginning with the Manifesto for Growth that former chairman and CEO Neville Isdell initiated and continuing on as current chairman and CEO Muhtar Kent advances his own strategy: the 2020 Vision (2020 Vision Press Release, 2009). The earlier examples centered upon the flagship branded product of The Coca-Cola Company, however, the more recent innovation strategies initiated under these leaders have been inclusive of all beverage categories. With the recent reality of changing consumer behaviors, new initiatives have been undertaken to harness these opportunities. The Coca-Cola Company has a strategy to capture sustainable growth with a specific focus on growing international markets in economies such as Brazil, Russia, India, and China. In this case, we look at how The Coca-Cola Company's actions to implement innovation-enabled strategies, establish global knowledge centers, common innovation processes, and reapplications of promising innovation across global markets have advantageously harnessed globalization for growth. These strategies have been recognized, and The Coca-Cola Company debuted for the first time on *BusinessWeek*'s The Most Innovative Companies list in 2009 at number

24, and then climbed five spots in 2010 to number 19 (Arndt, Einhorn, and Culpan, 2010).

INNOVATION-ENABLED STRATEGY

Upon his return to lead The Coca-Cola Company in 2004, now-retired Isdell began his turnaround of the company by tapping his top leaders to help craft a new strategy (Kelser, 2008). Dubbed the Manifesto for Growth, the key imperative was mapping a way to deliver sustainable growth for the future of The Coca-Cola Company and was underpinned by four key capabilities: brand marketing, franchise leadership, people development, and innovation (Kelser, 2008). The inclusion of innovation along with the company's historical expertise in marketing and franchise (bottling system) leadership was crucial to bringing a cultural focus to this capability. By making innovation a pillar of its strategic success, it became a key element in the geographic business unit plans needed to deliver The Coca-Cola Company's growth.

The follow-on strategy to the Manifesto for Growth—the 2020 Vision—was introduced publically by chairman and CEO Muhtar Kent in 2009 (2020 Vision Press Release, 2009). This new strategic work built upon that of its predecessor, specifically calling out the need for new innovations to reach its vision (2020 Vision Press Release, 2009). The 2020 Vision as shared by The Coca-Cola Company contains specific aspects of how innovation is to drive the portfolio pillar dimension of the strategy (2020 Vision, n.d.). This includes innovation that must be scalable, premium, and faster to market (2020 Vision, n.d.). The preceding examples of the two most recent strategies of The Coca-Cola Company from the last decade include innovation in key pillars. They illustrate the embedding of innovation as a critical capability for delivering business growth. With a strategy that emphasizes innovation in place, the additional elements are enabled for internal support and success to include global knowledge centers, process, and reapplication.

GLOBAL KNOWLEDGE CENTERS

The Coca-Cola Company began by exporting a single product developed in the United States —the beverage branded Coca-Cola—into countries across the world. This strategy worked well for decades, as the company successively entered new geographic locations. It was not until the Second World War that another product was added to The Coca-Cola Company's portfolio: Fanta. This product originated in The Coca-Cola

Company's European unit over 50 years after the original cola beverage (Product Descriptions, 2011). It was developed as a necessity for continuity of operations due to shortages of wartime ingredients. After the war ended, this product was expanded to other markets around the world.

Although Fanta was created in Europe more than 60 years ago, The Coca-Cola Company has recently been expanding this global knowledge base for innovation. The most recent example is the opening in 2009 of a new $90 million Global Innovation and Technology Center for Research and Development in Shanghai, China (News Release, 2009). This research and development center is now considered to be the most advanced in Asia for Coca-Cola's system, with expected benefits of speeding new innovations to market and defining new beverages for the world's largest beverage market, China (Leadership Viewpoints, 2009). Another research and development center for Europe is located in Brussels, Belgium and is considered the company's largest outside its headquarters in Atlanta, Georgia (A-point Planning & Execution, 2009). In addition, The Coca-Cola Company in 1993 formed an R&D subsidiary in Tokyo, Japan (Coca-Cola Tokyo R&D Co., Ltd.) to deliver product development to the Asia region; the center was separated from the U.S headquarters in Atlanta in 1995 (Sustainability: Corporate Responsibility, 2010). The Coca-Cola Company also has an additional research and development center in South America located in Rio de Janeiro, Brazil (In The News, 2009).

In addition to these technical development centers, The Coca-Cola Company has also built a global capability to collaborate with its beverage customers on innovation. There are three global cities having facilities called KO* Labs: North America in Atlanta, Europe in Brussels, and Asia in Shanghai. This was first raised during an interview with then-Chief Innovation Officer Danny Strickland, who shared a glimpse into the skunkworks-like KO Lab facility in Atlanta where customers get to see the company's cutting edge global innovation and also share ideas for new products (Martin, 2007). The Coca-Cola Company also has a KO Lab facility in Europe, located in Brussels alongside its research and development center (A-point Planning & Execution, 2009). In the same location as the recently constructed Global Innovation and Technology Center in Shanghai, there is also a KO Lab for customer collaboration complete with simulated retail and foodservice locations

---

* Editor's note: Stock symbol for The Coca-Cola Company sometimes used as a name abbreviation.

(Cooler Insights, 2010). As is clear from these examples, The Coca-Cola Company has invested in knowledge centers for technical and customer collaboration. This foundational strategic element of capable facilities is built on by the next enabler of its success in harnessing globalization, a single, worldwide innovation process.

COMMON INNOVATION PROCESS

It is one thing to have technical knowledge in the key geographic locations that The Coca-Cola Company operates in, but it is quite another for the people within this global system responsible for innovation to execute with discipline via a consistent process. Having this capability enables the third strategy of global reapplication. This is exactly what has been done. In the case of The Coca-Cola Company, this process has rigor and internal champions to drive it into the business (Knudson, 2008). The Coca-Cola Company has developed this process into a capability it calls the Common Innovation Framework, integral to collaboration within its internal, global business system (Weier, 2008). The Common Innovation Framework exists as a project management and business intelligence tool for its dispersed business units around the world (Weier, 2008). It is based upon the stages and gates methodology originally advanced over 25 years ago (Cooper, 1986). However, this process has now been automated. The innovation project begins as an idea from all sources and moves into refinement for development (Knudson, 2008). The innovation of new beverages, new equipment, and new packages all flows through the system's automated stages and gates process (as of 2008 in 50 countries) which is conveniently and rapidly accessed across the world from The Coca-Cola Company employees' Internet connections (Weier, 2008). The Common Innovation Framework also provides an innovation pipeline view; a view that allows resource prioritization against key projects (Weier, 2008). Former chairman and CEO Isdell identified this product development investment coordination as one of his key initial strategic priorities to get growth accelerated under his leadership at The Coca-Cola Company (Kelser, 2008).

This additional enabler of success of a consistent innovation framework globally is in place at The Coca-Cola Company. Built upon the dispersed knowledge centers in key global regions, the process provides both a common language for the innovation projects as well as a database offering a view of the overall pipeline. With these, the fourth element of reapplying innovations from one market to another can be realized.

GLOBAL REAPPLICATION

Reapplication, in the context of product innovation, is the reuse or repurposing of a new product or project from one geography or market into another. An obvious example of the above is the company's flagship brand, Coca-Cola. With this product sold in over 200 countries today, the cola originating in the United States has become the most successful beverage reapplication (Coca-Cola Company Information, 2011). Another more recent product to follow this path out of American success into global markets is Coca-Cola Zero. Coca-Cola Zero was developed and launched in 2005 nationally across the United States (Weier, 2008) and is today in 93 countries (Coke, Diet Coke, Coke Zero, Sprite & more, 2011). But the expansion of global knowledge centers points to new ideas that are developed in places other than the corporate home market, here in Atlanta, Georgia, USA. An exemplary case in point is Minute Maid Pulpy.

In Minute Maid Pulpy, The Coca-Cola Company has its fourteenth $1 billion dollar brand (Lee, 2011). First launched in 2005 for the Chinese market, Minute Maid Pulpy was developed in the emerging market, not at headquarters (Pulpy Joins Growing Roster of Billion Dollar Brands, 2011). The juice product has been reapplied in 18 markets, including Mexico (Pulpy Joins Growing Roster of Billion Dollar Brands, 2011). Grown in just over five years into a $1 billion dollar brand, Pulpy demonstrates the capability of The Coca-Cola Company to leverage its global knowledge centers via its innovation process to reach rapid scale on innovation. Returning to the earlier example of the fruit-flavored sparkling beverage brand, Fanta, The Coca-Cola Company was perhaps the original pioneer of such reapplication. Although grown over a longer period of time, Fanta is also a billion dollar brand of The Coca-Cola Company's global beverage portfolio. This ability to repurpose the product innovation in a focused disciplined way is another aspect of the company's successful global growth strategy for the future.

CLOSING REMARKS

This case has looked at the elements of strategic actions that The Coca-Cola Company has taken in its pursuit of growth across global beverage markets. The company has advanced innovation-enabled strategies, a network of global knowledge centers, a common innovation process, and reapplications of promising innovations across its geographic operations. Certainly, The Coca-Cola Company is a market leader in an established position as the world's largest beverage company and these new approaches appear to be driving growth as the company's stock has recently reached solid price levels and has been recognized for two straight years as a top global innovator. The future looks bright for The Coca-Cola Company's growth in all markets as an example of a U.S.-based company that has engineered how to successfully harness today's globalization.

REFERENCES

2020 Vision Press Release. (2009, Nov. 11). *The Coca-Cola Company Provides Roadmap for Achieving 2020 Vision at Analyst and Investor Event.* Retrieved from http://www.thecoca-colacompany.com/presscenter/nr_20091116_2020_vision.html

2020 Vision. (n.d.). *2020 Vision Roadmap for Winning Together: TCCC & Bottling Partners.* Retrieved from http://www.thecoca-colacompany.com/investors/pdfs/2020_vision.pdf

A-point Planning & Execution. (2009). *Media Visits to Brussels Tells the Coca-Cola Innovation Story.* Retrieved from http://www.a-point.be/Pages/Ko_Lab2.html

Arndt, M., Einhorn, B., and Culpan, T. (2010, April 25). The 50 Most Innovative Companies, *BusinessWeek* (4175), 34–40. Retrieved from http://www.businessweek.com

Bowman, Z. (2010). *Report: Currency fluctuations put plans for US Audi plant on hold,* http://www.autoblog.com/2010/06/29/report-currency-fluctuations-put-plans-for-u-s-audi-plant-on-h/, June 29.

Coca-Cola Company Information. (2011). *Growth, Leadership, Sustainability.* Retrieved from http://www.thecoca-colacompany.com/ourcompany/index.html

Coke, Diet Coke, Coke Zero, Sprite & more: Brands of The Coca-Cola Company. (2011). *Products.* Retrieved from http://www.thecoca-colacompany.com/brands/index.html

Cooler Insights. (2010, May 10). *Learning Coca-Cola's Secret Success Formula.* Retrieved from http://coolinsights.blogspot.com/2010/05/learning-coca-colas-secret-success.html

Cooper, R.G. (1986). *Winning at New Products: Accelerating the Process from Idea to Launch.* Cambridge, MA: Perseus.

Diaz, J. (2009). "How does inflation and currency fluctuation impact on your offshoring deal?," http://articlesadv.com/outsourcing/how-does-inflation-and-currency-fluctuation-impact-on-your-offshoring-deal-aRtIyuhe.html, March 18.

Entrepreneur Buddy (2010). *2011 Outsourcing Industry Predictions,* http://entrepreneur-buddy.net/global-outsourcing/2011-outsourcing-industry-predictions, November 23.

Hoffmann, L. (2010). Career opportunities, *Communications of the ACM,* November.

In The News. (2009). *A New Culture Of Innovation – November Investor Relation Presentation.* Retrieved from http://www.breakingawaythebook.com/press/06_Kaafarani_WEB CAST_V1

Kelser, G. (2008). How Coke's CEO aligned strategy and people to re-charge growth: An interview with Neville Isdell, *People & Strategy*, 31(2). Retrieved from http://www.chrs.net/images/chrs_papers/NevilleIsdellInterview.pdf

Knudson, L. (2008, April). Coca-Cola's new health kick, *Business Management*, 12. Retrieved from http://www.busmanagement.com/article/Coca-Colas-New-Health-Kick/

Kumar. S., Deivasigamani, A., and Omer, W. (2010). Knowledge for sale—The benefits and effects of off-shoring knowledge-based jobs in engineering, design, and R&D—A case study, *Knowledge Management Research & Practice Journal*, Operational Research Society/Palgrave, UK, 8: 4, December.

Leadership Viewpoints. (2009, June 23). *Remarks at the Nanching Bottling Plant Opening.* Retrieved from http://www.thecoca-colacompany.com/presscenter/viewpoints_kent_nanchang.html

Lee, J. and Kim, Y. (1999). Effect of partnership quality on IS outsourcing success: conceptual framework and empirical validation, *Journal of Management Information Systems*, 15: 4, March.

Lee, M. (2011, Feb. 1). *Coke adds billion dollar brand from China to portfolio*, Reuters. Retrieved From http://www.reuters.com/article/2011/02/01/idININdia-54554920110201

Martin, A. (2007, May 27). Coke struggles to keep up with nimble rivals. *The New York Times.* Retrieved from http://www.nytimes.com

McKenzie, D. and Henderson, M. (2010). *Trends in Outsourcing Emerging from the Great Recession*, http://www.technologybar.org/2010/10/trends-in-outsourcing-emerging-from-the-great-recession, October 13.

News Release. (2009, June 24). *Coca-Cola Accelerates Expansion in China: Two Plant Openings Mark New Wave of Investment in China.* Retrieved from http://www.thecoca-colacompany.com/presscenter/nr_20090624_two_plant_openings_in_china.html

Our Partnership History. (2008). Coca-Cola and The Olympic Games. Retrieved from http://www.thecoca-colacompany.com/heritage/pdf/Olympics_Partnership.pdf

Overby, S. (2009). *10 Outsourcing Trends to Watch in 2010*, www.cio.com, December 17.

Product Descriptions. (2011). Brand Name: Fanta. Retrieved from http://www.virtualvender.coca-cola.com/ft/index.jsp?brand_id=258

Pulpy Joins Growing Roster of Billion Dollar Brands Press Release. (2011, Feb. 1). *Minute Maid Pulpy Joins Growing Roster of Billion Dollar Brands for the Coca-Cola Company.* Retrieved from http://www.thecoca-colacompany.com/dynamic/press_center/2011/02/pulpy-joins-roster-of-billion-dollar-brands.html

Sustainability: Corporate Responsibility. (2010, July). *Coca-Cola Sustainability Report 2010.* Retrieved from http://www.thecoca-colacompany.com/citizenship/pdf/sustainability_reports/2010_japan_english.pdf

The Chronicle of Coca-Cola. (2011). A Symbol of Friendship. Retrieved from http://www.thecoca-colacompany.com/heritage/chronicle_symbol_friendship.html

Weier, M.H. (2008, July 19). Coke exploits collaboration technology to keep brand relevant, *InformationWeek*. Retrieved from http://www.informationweek.com/news/software/showArticle.jhtml?articleID=209100727

4

Gaining Competitive Advantage through E-Learning

Developing the human capital in an organization can lead to a competitive edge. Training and professional development are aligned with workforce development, strategic human capital, and succession planning. As today's organizations are global, the ability to quickly reach across the oceans to train and educate the organization's workforce is a critical success factor for achieving the mission and goals of the organization. The mechanism for accomplishing this knowledge transfer can be aptly met by the use of e-learning.

E-LEARNING TRENDS

Corporate training and development often take a blended learning approach. This involves the mixed use of face-to-face and online learning. For example, General Electric has an on-site executive leadership development program at Crotonville, New York, but also reinforces professional development through online learning such as webinars, virtual modules, and collaboration forums. Typically, the chief learning officer, in concert with the human resources and organizational development department, has the mandate to oversee the organizational learning and educational components of these types of workforce development programs. For example, Jody Hudson as the chief learning officer of the U.S. Nuclear Regulatory Commission (NRC) is in charge of the knowledge transfer and retention program, among other organizational learning components, at the NRC.

With e-learning, as well as other educational approaches, a model should be developed and applied to maximize learning effectiveness. One model can consist of three components: (1) knowledge-enabled; (2) learner-centered; and (3) community-access. Knowledge-enabled refers to providing ways to best leverage and transfer knowledge through teacher–student, student–student, and outside expert–student interactions. Learner-centered refers to focusing on the student and applying learning approaches that position the student at the hub of the learning engagement. Community-access refers to reaching out through social networking and other collaborative techniques to further engage the student.

E-learning is well-positioned to take advantage of such a model. E-learning is designed to be used as a learner-centered approach. The focus is on applying learning techniques to engage the student through one-on-one interactions with the teacher, group interactions through student community online forums, and online interactions with outside experts.

More sophisticated online techniques are being developed through virtual reality and artificial intelligence. For example, according to Clive Thompson (www.clivethompson.net), Professor Beverly Woolf at the University of Massachusetts-Amherst has developed autotutors using intelligent tutoring techniques that also sense emotion. Through expression detectors and wristbands that measure galvanic skin response, Professor Woolf equipped computers with these devices to gauge the student's engagement. Based on the level of engagement, the intelligent tutoring system could adjust its tutoring strategies to further engage the student for improved learning performance. According to Clive Thompson, the software was 80% accurate in sensing the student's moods and at the end of a 15-minute lesson, student users were three times more engaged than those working on regular unmodified computers.

Learning or courseware management systems, such as Blackboard (www.blackboard.com), WebTycho (*www.umuc.edu/grad/online/webtycho.shtml*), Moodle (moodle.org), and others, will look for ways to take advantage of social networking and Web 2.0 tools. Hooks for further collaboration and communication for student interaction will augment existing discussion forums, private messaging, group pages, and the like. Knowledge-based systems technology may also be used to have online ready access to a reservoir of expertise from outside the e-learning space. Blackboard's WIMBA and other personal videoconferencing tools like Skype (www.skype.com) will be integrated into e-learning platforms to accentuate the face-to-face interactions for enhancing the student's online learning experience. The use of virtual worlds (a later chapter in this book) and cloud computing may also play strong roles for learning engagement in the years ahead.

According to Ambient (www.ambientinsight.com), about 20% of the U.S. population has taken a course online. Certainly, many corporations have their own internal universities for training and professional development such as Motorola University and others. With travel costs rising and corporate training budgets decreasing over the recent years, e-learning is a cost-effective mechanism for reaching the corporate masses worldwide. Anytime, anyplace (asynchronous communication) is a prudent way of delivering course content to working adults.

SUMMARY OF THE "EMERGING TECHNOLOGIES FOR ONLINE COURSES" SURVEY RESULTS*

In order to get a sense of the current and expected usage for online instructional technologies for college and university courses, a survey was conducted during April 2010 by Jay Liebowitz, John Aje, and Steve Knode in the Graduate School of Management & Technology at the University of Maryland University College (UMUC). The focus of the survey was to better understand which emerging technologies are being used or will be used in the next two to three years for online teaching. Most of the 90 responses were from the Maryland Distance Learning Association listserv, DEOS listserv, and through the authors' personal contacts in the e-learning world. The sample size is rather small, but perhaps these survey results may provide some clarity on these issues.

Based on the survey results, the respondents were from a variety of teaching disciplines. Education (32%) was the leader, followed by humanities, other (e.g., nursing, counseling, etc.), sciences, management, technology, and arts. The technologies that were most familiar to the respondents, in order, were: Web 2.0 tools, e-books, virtual worlds, mobile computing, and cloud computing. Those technologies least familiar to the respondents were, in order of familiarity: visual data analysis, intelligent agents, software-as-a-service (SaaS), and semantic Web.

Of those technologies currently used in online teaching, Web 2.0 tools (e.g., blogs, wikis, social networking sites, podcasts, vodcasts, etc.) and

---

* http://umuc.edu/library/research_pubs/announcements/EmergingTechnologiesSummary2010.pdf

e-books were the favorites, with Web 2.0 tools taking the largest usage share (77%). Cloud computing (28%) and mobile computing (24%) were also being used, but to a much lesser degree. The other technologies were hardly being used currently in the respondents' online courses.

However, there were technologies, other than those listed, that were actively being used now in the online courses. The most recurring ones were: Skype, learning objects/course management systems, and YouTube. With respect to future usage of some of the emerging technologies in the coming two to three years, those cited in order were: Web 2.0 tools (81%), e-books (78%), virtual worlds (50%), mobile computing (50%), and cloud computing (47%). Intelligent agents, visual data analysis, SaaS, and semantic web, in decreasing order, were cited as those not expected to be used much in online teaching in the next two to three years. Simulations were indicated by the respondents as another possible favorite for usage in the next two to three years in online teaching.

In determining the top educational technologies that the respondents found to be the most effective for online use, as measured by student learning outcomes, those frequently cited were: Web 2.0 technologies, learning objects, videoconferencing/vodcasts/podcasts, synchronous chat and asynchronous discussion threads, wikis, blogs, screencasts, virtual worlds, and simulations. In terms of how these educational technologies were best used in online teaching, the frequent responses were: making lectures more interactive, collaboration (such as the use of wikis), reflective learning journals, RSS feeds to allow students to stay abreast of research in their fields, allowing student interaction, and student review of content material.

The top lessons learned in applying these educational technologies in online teaching were: students are more willing to participate when they are comfortable or familiar with certain types of technology; students still have to take time to "learn;" the technologies should not get in the way of the learning process; prepare well in advance of implementation; it is essential to maintain an online presence; social presence is increased with videoconferencing and social media; there is a need for institutional support for questions dealing with technologies; and technologies have to be simple and enjoyable for students to use.

With respect to the educational technologies being cost-effective for the institution in terms of online course usage, 84% indicated "Yes" and 16% "No." Of those who replied "No," a major reason cited was not having a serviceable platform to incorporate these technologies. In terms of whether the current online courseware will be used in one's online courses in the next three years, 71% replied "Yes" and 29% said "No." Part of the reason for those replying "No" was due to not having the ability to have links or hooks to incorporate some of these technologies into the existing courseware.

The next case study discusses the genesis of e-learning and faculty development at the University of Maryland University College.

Case Study: Rethinking Training and Professional Development on a Global Scale: A Tale of Three Cities

Richard Schumaker
University of Maryland University College

Conventional wisdom teaches us that professional development and workforce training programs are essential if an organization is going to be successful in today's global, digital, and often tumultuous economic environment. To appeal to this demand, thousands of commercial ads for seminars, webinars, and veritable curricula on workforce training are listed on Google, our universal muse.

However, conventional wisdom generally masks more than it reveals; most of these commercial references to training programs remind us that organizations need training, but seldom do they really explain, beyond truisms and clichés, what kind of training is needed, how it is to be implemented, or, in most cases, why it is so important.

Thus, managers and executives search for assistance in improving their employees' performance by reading articles, looking at websites, and hearing publicity about the latest breakthroughs in professional training. Yet they are often left hanging, wondering, "What do these programs really do …?" Or, "How can I possibly choose between these offerings that all sound the same?"

In order to explore the deeper question of why training and professional development are so important, this case study focuses on a single global institution and illustrates the precise steps taken during a specific period of time (roughly 1996–2002) to implement comprehensive training in global operations, spanning many continents, languages, and ethnicities. Because of the extreme heterogeneity of this institution, this case study has considerable relevance for senior managers and executives who are responsible for many different kinds of global institutions.

Specifically, this case study concerns an educational institution that is now the largest public university in the United States, the University of Maryland University College (UMUC). This school, along with the University of Maryland at College Park, the University of Maryland at Baltimore, Towson University, and others, is part of the University System of Maryland (http://en.wikipedia.org/wiki/University_System_of_Maryland). Founded in 1947 to meet the needs of an evolving postwar society, until recently UMUC was located on the College Park campus and was, for most campus visitors, indistinguishable from the University of Maryland at College Park. Over the last 10 years, UMUC has outgrown its original facilities and now has locations all over Prince George's County, including an impressive new Academic Center in Largo, Maryland.

Our case study focuses on the choices that a few superlative senior leaders made starting in 1996 as advances in information technology opened the door to offering college courses online. These administrators, Drs. Nicholas Allen, Joseph Arden, and John Floyd, working from the university's three divisional administrative centers in the Maryland suburbs of Washington D.C., Heidelberg, and Tokyo made key decisions in a time of considerable historical and political flux between 1996 and roughly 2002. These decisions derived from five principles that can serve as guides for the creation of successful professional development programs to achieve stable organizational growth and quality performance.

Before we explore these five principles, let's establish the basic demographic profile of UMUC. In 2011, UMUC has roughly 95,000 students (unduplicated headcount) and approximately 4,500 professors. Commencement exercises in the United States are so large that they fill the Comcast Center on the College Park campus, twice in a single day. There are also parallel commencement exercises in Japan and Germany. In 2011, more than 8,700 degrees were awarded. The ratio of stateside to overseas students is very roughly 60/40, with the larger number being within the United States. The average age of a UMUC student is about 30. Roughly half of the students at this school are white; roughly 30% are African American. In 2001, almost 74,000 students took at least one online class. Of UMUC's total students, over 30,000 of them are associated with the U.S. military in some way (http://www.umuc.edu/ip/factsheet-10.shtml).

Now that we have established the demographics of our case study, let's look at the five principles that should guide managers and senior executives as they plan and implement their professional training programs.

THE FULL MONTY PRINCIPLE

When planning or rethinking one's current training program, it is very tempting to simply fix what is obviously broken or attend to what is obviously and immediately useful. However, rather than being seduced by quick fixes and partial solutions, it is critical that training programs be resolutely comprehensive: more precisely, training and development, to be successful, should affect all members of an organization at every moment of their career paths.

In the case of UMUC, this meant mapping out a five-stage program of distinct but overlapping training and development courses. This was a very complex task because the thousands of professors and administrators in this organization were spread all over the world with large clusters in areas as diverse as metropolitan Washington D.C., Tokyo, Okinawa, Frankfurt, throughout the United Kingdom, and in the vernacular of this institution "downrange," that is, the various areas where U.S. troops were stationed.

Also the range of academic qualification at this university was immense, ranging from world-class scholars with relationships to St. John's College, Oxford, Johann Wolfgang Goethe University, Frankfurt, and Ca' Foscari in Venice to third-year graduate students spending a year in Europe and teaching for UMUC to earn a little extra money. Due to UMUC's global presence, teaching for UMUC was very attractive to authors such as Donna Leon or Erica Jong who taught in Vicenza and Heidelberg, respectively. To prepare such a diverse group of teachers for online teaching, a sequence of training programs was developed to cover all levels of college instructors at all aspects of their career lifecycles at UMUC.

First, a baseline training course was needed. Considerable patient planning was required to develop a five-week course that would meet the needs of the geographically dispersed instructors living in Bethesda, Kabul, as well as at airbases in Germany and Navy submarine stations at La Maddelena, Italy.

Second, once the baseline skills and techniques were communicated, a more sophisticated and specialized series of workshops and tutorials needed to be developed. In many ways, this part of the training was even more difficult to plan, organize, and implement because one has to work less on pedagogical generalities of online instruction than on the specific, sometimes arcane, concepts of each academic field. In the case of UMUC, in order to guarantee academic rigor, it was crucial to teach faculty to use a dauntingly complicated online library, something that in 1996 and 1997 many educators did not know existed.

Third, an intervention strategy was needed in case the baseline course or the workshops did not work. What if a professor who had passed the baseline course became confused or perplexed three weeks into his online course? A coaching program was designed for these eventualities.

Fourth, a sophisticated peer mentoring program was developed that drew on the experience and sense of purpose of the more experienced faculty who assisted professors who were "the new kids on the block."

Finally, to ensure that this university without borders did not become a soulless labyrinth, Dr. Nicholas Allen devised the idea of a summer leadership institute where the best of the best, the top guns of this academic universe, would meet in August to exchange ideas and listen to world-class educators. The attendees of the UMUC Summer Institute would then return to Japan, Italy, Spain, the former Yugoslavia, or wherever they were teaching and impart their wisdom and collegial experience.

THE EXISTENTIAL PRINCIPLE

Successful training programs must not be abstract; they must suit the true needs of the actual people participating in them. The genius of the UMUC administrators in 1996 was that not only did they create an architectural framework for their multitiered program, but also they understood the importance of the human factor. They knew that the heterogeneity and global footprint of their university would not allow "just-for-the-United States" approaches: it would be crucial to design a program for their global, diverse, and often contentious faculty. Above all, the training personnel—the trainers, course writers, and managers—needed to be selected extremely carefully. More precisely, the criteria for choosing training personnel in this digital global environment must match the needs of one's organization.

In the case of UMUC, in the very early days of their professional development programs, IT trainers were chosen. This seemed to make a lot of sense: wasn't UMUC teaching the use of a course management system, essentially software? Didn't the IT trainers have the best backgrounds to identify problems and explain them in a serious rigorous fashion? After a very short period of time, the UMUC administration found that engineers had a very difficult time understanding the perspective of someone who did not know a bit from a byte. The computer engineers were also less than comfortable about teaching professors who were doing research on the Franco-Prussian War or Garibaldi. The trainers with an IT background were also somewhat ill at ease with the often idiosyncratic personalities of the social scientists and creative writers who were teaching classes for UMUC. On the other hand, trainers with backgrounds in literature, philosophy, foreign languages, and government not only enjoyed the give and take of the liberal arts teachers but, also they could pick up the technological dimension of online teaching easily and could communicate with panache and intellectual rigor. Finally, UMUC learned to choose its trainers on sociological grounds. With so many of UMUC's students and many of its teachers connected to the military, choosing trainers with extensive military background worked extremely well.

Moreover, UMUC was extremely fortunate to be able to draw on the experience of faculty with training backgrounds in the United States and military and diplomatic corps. They were chosen to prepare the UMUC faculty to teach online because they had academic knowledge of professional development and real-world experience; they could relate to the faculty scattered all over the planet because they were well-traveled people and had experience teaching UMUC students. For example, Richard Powers, who currently lives in Stuttgart and Amsterdam is an Army Reserve Lt. Colonel who had trained troops by jumping from airplanes at Fort Benning, participated in NATO, REFORGER, and WINTEXT/CIMEX exercises, and graded artillery firings at Grafenwoehr at 4:00 a.m. on snowy November mornings. Another trainer, Andreas Rambow, lives in Brussels, Belgium and had previously traveled the globe with the German *Bundeswehr*. Another of the trainers, Deborah Hullet, is a linguist who lives in Texas and managed to balance raising five children with work assignments in Australia, Europe, and Asia. Yet another trainer, Jane Burman-Holtom, currently lives in South Florida and has a background in advertising, public relations, project management, and consulting for organizations as diverse as international companies, state universities, and agencies. She was born and raised near Stratford-upon-Avon. Among them, they speak nine languages and bring a world of experience to their professional development courses at UMUC.

All of these people are cosmopolitan, infinitely stable, moderate, educational idealists who have trained and educated thousands of UMUC faculty in the art of online discourse during the growth surge of UMUC between 1996 and 2011.

THE SOCRATIC PRINCIPLE

The third of our principles deals with the kind of discourse fostered in the UMUC training courses and programs. Traditionally, training is very straightforward: material is structured and prewritten; the trainer is the all-knowing authority; trainees are processed rapidly and rather quickly through a course or a program.

In the early days of the UMUC program, something like this was tried, but it backfired. In fact, UMUC had three different forms of resistance to its early training programs, especially the mandatory ones. First, faculty detested the very idea of being forced to take training courses. As someone once said, "From the time I was five, I was one of the best students in my class. I went to private schools in high school and college. I finished my PhD at 27 and have been teaching for 23 years. I have never had a course in teaching; my professors were interested in answers, not instruction. Why should I now be "trained?" Why can't I work out on my own how to teach online?"

Second, even if they accepted the idea of training, they disliked scripted programmed training; consequently, UMUC had to change its mode of instruction and rethink things such as tone, syntax, forms of courtesy, and vocabulary.

Finally, online teaching was so new that no one had a clear idea of a precise training model. Many educators were fiercely skeptical. One of the UMUC trainers, Richard Powers, related his experience at the ESSE (European Society for the Study of English) 1995 conference in Glasgow, where in the midst of giving a presentation on teaching *Othello* online, the contingent of German tenured professors literally stormed out of the room, evoking total scorn for the American professor: "Bah Humbug," they seemed to say.

In essence, it was necessary for UMUC to invent a new form of training, emphasizing give and take and spirited discussion of very diverse points of view. Because the diverse international groups of professors were comfortable with them, it was necessary to accept flights of fancy, occasional irrationality, and digression. Typical corporate training courses avoid conflict; these professors accepted it as natural and necessary to their professional environment.

Over time, as they studied the training sessions, the administrators and trainers at UMUC came to understand the needs and values of their faculty better. This meant that there would be clashes, sidebars, and ideological debates between participants in the training sessions. In the early days of the program, there were many disruptions, often caused by overanxious trainers trying to keep to the schedule, to be trainers in the conventional sense. In time, the trainers learned to relax, enjoy these heated discussions, and rejoice in the intelligence and pedagogical passions of the professors.

PLAN FOR CHANGE

Most of the time professional development programs aim to meet precise empirical needs. For example, a company sends an executive to France and prepares her by sending her to a language school. Or a manager is having trouble understanding or tracking daily operational realities, so he is given a tutorial in PeopleSoft. Such remedies have obvious value for precise well-defined needs, but UMUC's needs change every time a moderately important technological change occurs, which is weekly. Thus, it is crucial to build continual professional development possibilities into the very fiber of the programs. This is done in several ways.

In the baseline training course, taken as soon as most professors are hired, the value of continued professional growth is presented and discussed. Also, precise future pathways for how this is to be achieved are presented. All faculty are given development plans or roadmaps as to how they can improve as online teachers. A good example of this concerns the use of technology in interacting with individual students. Because the standard U.S. college lecturer has little experience with using technology to discuss ideas in any meaningful way with individual students, faculty are guided in this skill carefully and gradually. For roughly a year, the UMUC professors work at learning to transpose their basic courses by inserting static images, audio feedback, and using the vast resources of the online library. After practice with online learning at this level, if they like, they can work on using multimedia and video in increasingly sophisticated formats. As they develop, they can take both pedagogical and technical workshops, getting feedback from their trainers and from their departmental specialists in these areas.

For the professors, the arc from a low-tech to high-tech college classroom is a rewarding important experience that over time often leads to professional and personal renewal. For the UMUC training team, the courses that make the improvements possible are systematically planned, constantly refined, and the source of great conviction and pride. Ultimately, it is this belief in the school, its mission, and its future which is the deepest of the five principles addressed in this case study.

ADDRESS THE VISION

Above all, UMUC's training and development program is grounded in the vision and mission of the school, which is centered on being one of the world's great teaching institutions, respecting the working adults who form most of its student body, and offering courses that help adult students achieve important and practical "job skills," as well as exposure to the fundamental legacies and values of society, culture, and traditions.

Each training program at UMUC, described in Principle 1 of this case study, integrates this vision and sense of purpose into everything that is taught. The core group of 15 trainers thinks hard about how to intelligently communicate the UMUC mission in its training courses. This belief in the importance of purpose and vision is what separates this form of training from the more mechanical and pragmatic training that one encounters in most commercial enterprises and in many academic tracts on professional development. Arguably, UMUC's astute integration of broad ethical values into "mandatory training" is the deepest lesson to be learned from this important educational enterprise.

CONCLUSION

Thus, this case study is the story of three senior administrators in three different, widely separated cities: Nicholas Allen, Joe Arden, and John Floyd operated from administrative centers in the Maryland suburbs of Washington D.C., Heidelberg, Germany, and Tokyo, Japan in the early days of the online revolution in education. They could have taken the easy path and rejected the idea of training as being too costly, or they could have suggested a quick-fix "two hours and done" software training. Instead, they chose to set up a comprehensive training program touching each faculty member in many different ways; they chose to think through how the training course would be communicated to the faculty and, above all, why this kind of professional development would be important for UMUC professors. Respecting the deeper professional needs of their employees, the administrators under study here made a choice, a hard choice, about the values that would be instilled at this university as their professors joined the institution, after they had taught a few classes, and as they become very skilled instructors navigating this revolution in global teaching and learning. Few doubt the wisdom of this difficult choice made years ago in three very different cities.

SUMMARY

E-Learning will continue to play a more important role in training and education in organizations worldwide. Senior leaders must leverage these technologies to nurture their human capital toward building a continuous learning organization. In the coming years, personalization and mobile learning (using mobile computing devices) will be major trends in the e-learning space. Senior leaders, especially the chief learning officer, vice president of human resources, and the chief technology officer, must think about how best to apply these approaches for their organization's value-added benefits.

5

Gaining Competitive Advantage through Social Networking

Collaboration and communication are the buzzwords being echoed in the halls of management. If employees could connect with others better, especially those employees outside their own departments, the possibility of innovative and creative ideas may generate. In social networking parlance, these "weak ties," those relationships fostered through connecting with others outside one's own area of expertise, may increase innovation to the organization (Liebowitz, 2010). Having ways to reach out to one's customer base may also generate new ideas and improve customer relationships. For example, Hallmark Cards has online communities where the general public can suggest new ideas for greeting cards. This information helps build the knowledge base of the organization and may promote new products or services.

According to the January 2011 issue of *IEEE Spectrum*, social networking was listed as the second top technology for the decade (smartphones were listed as #1). Making connections is at the heart of business, and social networking is a simple medium to allow these connections to develop. According to Ariel Bleicher of *IEEE Spectrum*, as of December 2010, there were about 540 million Facebook users who spent about 700 billion minutes on the Facebook site every month; if it were a country, it would be the third most populous in the world. Many social networking sites have been developed over the years (MySpace, Flickr, YouTube, LinkedIn, Friendster, Orkut, Twitter, Facebook Connect, etc.), and there are newer ones being created such as Ning, Google Me, and others. In 2010, the *Time* Person of the Year was Mark Zuckerberg, the Facebook cofounder. A movie called *The Social Network* about the Facebook experience also appeared at the end of 2010. Certainly, social networking (as well as geo-location-based services such as Foursquare, SimpleGeo, and others) are upon us and will continue to grow in the years ahead.

INNOVATION THROUGH SOCIAL NETWORKING

There have been many examples of social networking leading to an organizational advantage through innovation. Solvay, a pharmaceutical and chemical company in Belgium, is using maps based on social network analysis to increase its innovation efforts and for succession planning (Liebowitz, 2007). IBM uses social network analysis to survey the informal interactions between various groups of employees to promote the creation of new ideas (Liebowitz, 2007). CGIAR (Consultative Group on International Agricultural Research), funded through the World Bank, uses ShareFairs, blogs, wikis, and other collaborative techniques to share, transfer, and generate new ideas as related to agricultural research (http://ictkm.cgiar.org). Rob Cross and Robert Thomas' 2009 book titled *Driving Results Through Social Networks: How Top Organizations Leverage Networks for Performance and Growth* is filled with examples of how social networks are stimulating innovation.

Now, let's say a word or two about social or organizational network analysis (SNA/ONA). This technique is used by many organizations, for example, to map knowledge flows and knowledge gaps for improving collaboration and innovation. SNA/ONA also allows organizations to identify different brokering roles of their employees and management. These roles could be central connectors, boundary spanners, peripheral specialists, and others. SNA/ONA provides a sound approach to get a glimpse of the organization from looking at the network structures.

SNA/ONA tries to determine the shortest path between two nodes. It is based on link analysis and graph theory. Various statistics are calculated in the background, and a visualization of the social network maps can be developed. One tool that is often used is called UCINET-Netdraw (it can be found at: http://www.analytictech.com/products.htm). There are several other SNA/ONA tools (they can also be found at the International Network for Social Network Analysis site at www.insna.org). Figure 5.1 shows an example of a social network map, using NetMiner (www.netminer.com) depicting the flow of strategic knowledge through the organization. The data were collected by surveys, e-mail traffic, and weblogs. This figure

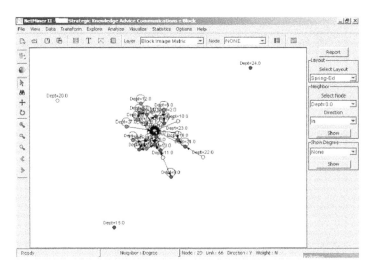

FIGURE 5.1
Strategic knowledge flow through a company's departments.

shows that most of the departments are nestled together with respect to strategic knowledge flow; however, there are a few outlying departments (Departments 24, 20, and 15). They do not seem to be in the flow of strategic knowledge in the organization. And, what if Department 24 is actually the Strategic Planning Department for the organization? Then, there should be some realignments to be sure that at least Department 24 (and most likely, the other two departments) is in the flow of strategic knowledge.

Social network analysis can also show relationships or the flow of knowledge between different levels in the organization, whether staff, manager, director, executive, or other. Figure 5.2 is an example that shows the larger cube being non-management employees and the smaller cube being senior management. This figure portrays the flow of process knowledge between the junior- and senior-level employees in an organization.

Digital Marketing Strategy

Certainly, social networking is part of the overarching digital marketing strategy for an organization. In today's world, having a "digital footprint," is vital for any organization. According to Wikipedia (http://en.wikipedia.org/wiki/Digital_footprint):

> A digital footprint is a trail left by an entity's interactions in a digital environment, including their usage of TV, mobile phone, Internet and World

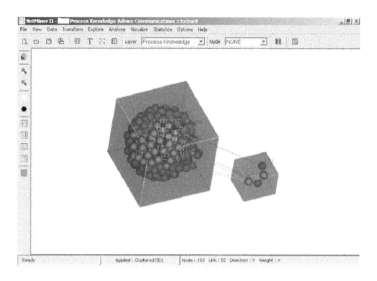

FIGURE 5.2
Junior-senior employee process knowledge flows.

Wide Web, mobile web, and other devices and sensors. Digital footprints provide data on what an entity has performed in the digital environment, and are valuable in assisting behavioral targeting, personalization, targeted marketing, digital reputation, and other social media or social graphing services.

To be competitive, organizations must be proactive in their digital marketing strategy. For example, the use of data, text, and web mining techniques can help identify hidden patterns and relationships that may help in customer segmentation, customer relationship management, and targeted marketing. Recommender systems can identify similar products that may interest the buyer, such as Amazon's approach to suggesting what others have bought when they have purchased your item. Walmart has used data mining software over the years for demand forecasting. According to Adam Singer of The Future Buzz (http://thefuturebuzz.com/2010/01/04/digital-marketing-strategy/), there are 12 common problems that may occur in developing a digital marketing strategy:

1. Lack of understanding what image they are trying to project
2. No path to acquire and grow an audience
3. No cohesion of content
4. Placating executives by executing their bad ideas
5. Having to dumb things down for the team
6. Living and dying by data

7. Trying to reach the wrong group
8. Misunderstanding the importance of content
9. No plan to actually reach anyone in the first place
10. No difference from others
11. No forming of relationships/alliances
12. Lack of influencers on your team

Organizations must be cognizant of these potential problems and develop a digital marketing strategy that is aligned with the strategic vision, mission, and goals of the organization. Organizations must be proactive, and if not, they could be left behind as stated by Brian Pasch in November 2010 (http://automotive-seo.ning.com/profiles/blogs/fiat-dealers-failed-seo-101):

> I bring this up because of the latest jump ball in search marketing was the assignment of Fiat dealerships. 128 Fiat "Studios" (dealers) were publicly announced a few weeks ago and it is amazing how many of these franchise owners have not started a digital marketing strategy to lock-in organic search placement before the third parties come to play. For many of these dealers, they had a strong "heads up" in September that they would be getting a franchise. Over 70% of the dealers have not even purchased their domain names.

Looking Ahead

According to Ashley Friedlein (http://econsultancy.com/us/blog/7014-digital-marketing-trends-2011-by-econsultancy-ceo-ashley-friedlein),these are some of the major trends that will occur in the near term. In the near term, we will see social media evolving into a more social business. Location services coupled with social media will also probably increase. The mobile web will continue to grow and mobile search companies will also play a more major role. Gaming will also increase in terms of social gaming and how it affects marketing. Cloud computing will grow as well, and companies such as Salesforce.com are planning on playing a larger role in the cloud computing market.

In order to appreciate how companies are using social media for their competitive advantage, Sandeep Patnaik at Gallup and Robinson provides an overview of trends and applications in the use of social networking sites. Afterwards, Dr. Matt North associate professor of information technology leadership at Washington & Jefferson College discusses eBay in terms of social networking as a specific case study.

Going Social: Case Studies of Successful Social Media Marketing

Sandeep Patnaik
Gallup & Robinson, Inc.

INTRODUCTION

In recent years there has been a tremendous increase in the growth and popularity of social media networks. A significant majority of people with access to the Internet are active participants in these sites. There is growing evidence that users of social networking sites now include people of various age groups with a significant number of active users 40 years or older with women outnumbering men in popular sites such as Facebook. This virtual explosion in social media has naturally attracted the attention of marketers and there has been a continuous effort to leverage the reach and access of social networks for brand promotion in terms of actual sales and customer service. Marketing in social media channels, however, presents its unique set of challenges. The dynamic and interactive nature of social media demands that marketers have to be constantly engaged with the target market. So apart from money, successful social media marketing requires significant investment in time and creative input. The following sections discuss some illustrative case studies of businesses creatively using social media channels. We have primarily focused on the two most dominant social media networks, Facebook and Twitter, to highlight the success stories in a few select categories. The cases illustrate a range of creative strategies employed by organizations to rise over the clutter of competition and gain greater competitive advantage in the marketplace. The new media have forced organizations to constantly think outside the box and in the process have redefined the very concept of marketing. Finally we point to some future trends in social media marketing and suggest strategies about how organizations can deal with them to their best advantage.

Social media loosely refers to a wide spectrum of web-based and mobile applications that enable social interaction across geographical boundaries mainly through user-generated content. In recent years, particularly in the last couple of years, there has been an exponential growth not only in the number of social media networks but also in the sociodemographic attributes of their user base. Unlike in previous years, social networking sites are no longer the exclusive preserve of the younger generation. In fact the number of social media users aged 65 years or older almost doubled in 2010; currently about a quarter of people in that age group actively participate in a social networking site.[1]

ComScore's comprehensive 2010 review of digital usage[2] reveals that although Google and Yahoo sites remain the most visited web properties in the United States (with approximately 180 million visitors a month) social networking now ranks as the second most engaging activity at 14.4% of time spent online. Facebook has captured the number one ranking by *time spent* in August 2010, accounting for 12.3% of time spent online in the United States.

The report notes that 9 out of every 10 U.S. Internet users have visited a social networking site each month with the average Internet user spending more than 4.5 hours per month on these sites. Interestingly, women spent more time on these sites (16.8%) compared to men who spent 12% of their time on social networking sites. As well, the 2010 review observes that there is a continuing decline in time spent on regular web portals and a corresponding increase in time spent at social networking sites.

These and other data make it increasingly clear that social networking has become integral to the daily life of a majority of Americans with access to the Internet. Equally important, the age distribution in social media sites has become much less skewed than before. More than half of active users in social media sites are now 40 years old or older.[3] There is a continuing trend of older, more financially stable people actively participating and uploading content into the social media sites. As well, women are much more active in social networks than in other online activities.

MARKETING IN SOCIAL MEDIA

The rising popularity of social media networks has naturally attracted marketers keen to leverage the ease of access and technological capabilities of these sites to gain a competitive edge in the marketplace. Marketers who were previously frustrated by the decline in effectiveness of traditional marketing channels such as direct-to-customers (DTC) communications or even print/TV advertisements are now eager to capitalize on the ready access that social network sites provide.

The rising interest in social networking sites as viable vehicles for marketing is also reflected in the money being spent to advertise on social networks. According to *eMarketer* spending on advertisements on social networking sites has increased from $1.40 billion in 2009 to a projected $3 billion in 2011, a nearly 50% increase.[4]

However, notwithstanding the growing levels of advertising dollars invested in social media, it is important to recognize that money is only a small part of the investment required for successful social marketing. Most social media marketers recognize that paid advertising is only a fraction of the spending. Social media marketing requires a holistic approach and requires a significant amount of effort to be invested in brand-building activities through blogs, podcasts, tweets, and the like. The basic mantra for success in social media is that each campaign has to be presented in a unique and engaging manner.

Some brands have managed to develop highly successful and creative campaigns to more fully engage the customer with the brand. A good example of a creative campaign has been devised by the Oreo brand. Each week, the site randomly selects photographs of a few of its fans and advertises them on its home page. As well, the site announces a "Fan of the Week" on its status update. By promoting its "fans" on its website, the brand seeks to develop a closer rapport with its customers.[5] As an excellent social media marketer, the brand not only listens but also acts on what it hears from its target audience. For example in 2010 it created a Pandora radio station out of the popular songs voted on by its fans, indicative of the importance that it accords to its loyal fan base.

Similarly, Red Bull's Facebook page contains extreme sports and is designed to attract a younger demographic. This is congruent with its brand image and also helps its targeted customers identify with its marketing message.

The trend toward increased involvement of marketers in social networks is predicted to be even greater in the immediate future. According to the 2011 Digital Marketing Outlook, published by Society of Digital Agencies (SoDA) more than 95% of a sample pool of brand marketers, marketing agencies, and so on, plan to use some form of social media in 2011.[6]

Table 5.1 suggests that although marketers still give top priority to their own sites, social networking sites are increasingly getting to be as important. At the very, least social media sites are deemed to be crucial to help drive traffic to the main corporate site.

Several independent studies have found that a majority of U.S. marketers are currently using social media. For example, a recent

TABLE 5.1

Digital Media Channels Used by Organizations 2011

	Brand Marketers (%)	Agencies (%)
Facebook	76	96
Twitter	69	89
MySpace	5	9
Blogs	57	75
Other Social Media sites	29	40
Corporate Website	80	81

Source: 2011 DMO published by SoDA.

survey on social media usage in Fortune 500 companies conducted by the University of Massachusetts Dartmouth Center for Marketing Research (2010) found that 60% of the Fortune 500 companies now have regularly updated Twitter accounts. As well, 56% of these companies have an active presence on Facebook.[7] Furthermore, unlike in the past, organizations are currently much more proactive and engaged in the social media arena. A recent Social Media Marketing Industry Report (2010)[8] found that 86% of marketers spend at least 6 hours or more each week with 12.5% of marketers spending more than 20 hours each week on social media. The survey listed the following reasons cited by these organizations as their top reasons for using social media:

1. Generated exposure for business: 85%
2. Resulted in new business partnership: 56%
3. Helped in raising the search rankings: 54%
4. Helped in selling products and services: 48%

The above responses indicate that a large number of business are increasingly turning to social media networks to improve their brand image and also to market their offerings effectively.

CASE STUDIES OF SUCCESSFUL USE OF SOCIAL MEDIA

Considering the relatively short history of social networking sites, it is remarkable to find a large number of organizations have successfully used them as platforms to promote their brands, support customers, and increase business. Some of the most successful marketing campaigns have involved creative use of Facebook and Twitter. Facebook particularly has developed into a very hospitable platform for a wide array of marketing initiatives by diverse organizations.

One of the earliest and most successful social media campaigns, called the Fiesta Movement, was launched by Ford in April 2009 to promote its Fiesta model. In an innovative strategy, the company selected 100 top bloggers and gave each of them a Fiesta to use for the next six months. In return they (i.e., the bloggers or "agents") were required to upload a video on YouTube about the car along with an independent account of their experience with the Fiesta, on their blogs. The Fiesta Movement campaign was a tremendous success. The 700 videos created by the "agents" generated 6.5 million views on YouTube and created more than 3.4 million impressions on Twitter. Photos of the car uploaded onto Flickr were viewed more than 670,000 times. The campaign generated considerable buzz about the vehicle with more than 50,000 U.S. consumers (90% of whom did not previously own a Ford vehicle) wanting more information about the Fiesta. Ford sold 10,000 units in the first six days of sales.[9]

Encouraged by the tremendous success of its Fiesta social media initiative, Ford drilled deeper into the social media space to obtain direct consumer experience.[10] For example, data obtained from websites such as www.syncmyride.com—an owner-to-owner forum that had logged complaints about the quality of the automated voice on Ford's SYNC system—helped Ford to tweak the software to make the voice less loud.

The exponential growth of interest in social networking as legitimate business channels has coincided with the popularity of Facebook. In just a couple of years Facebook's active user base has grown from about 100 million in 2008 to about 600 million users in January, 2011. Not surprisingly some of the most outstanding instances of success in social media marketing have taken place via Facebook.

Clorox is a good example of a brand that tweaked its social media advertising to generate optimal awareness and revenue. In 2010 the company hosted a Green Works webpage. The target audience was females aged 25–34 and the goal was to increase the awareness of the Green Works brand of environmentally friendly products. Clorox targeted Facebook users who had listed "clean" and "green" in their Facebook profiles.[11] A follow-up study by Nielsen found that thanks to the campaign, the "intent to purchase" the Green Works detergent among Facebook users increased by 7%. The study also found that the campaign resulted in a significant 12% increase in awareness of the brand.

The social marketing strategy adopted by Bob Evans, a restaurant and retail food products company operating nearly 600 restaurants in 38 states and with a revenue of $1.7 billion, is illustrative of how online marketing can drive traffic to physical stores. In July 2010, the company on its Facebook page announced that it would give away its "Sweet Potato Fries" during National French Fries Day. The campaign was a huge success as it generated nearly 85 million digital impressions of which 6 million were social. During the two-week period the number of people who "liked" the Bob Evans Facebook page rose from 22,000 to over 40,000 and the campaign had a return on investment of between 200 and 300%.[12]

Similarly, Starbucks has been at the forefront of using social media in its marketing ventures. The company has an estimated 20+ million followers on Facebook (and about 1.5 million followers on Twitter) and regularly provides discounts as well as promotional offers through these networks.[13] Interestingly, the company has refrained from using the channel for any hard marketing sell. Instead the effort has been to create a Starbucks community feeling that promotes open community-oriented discussion. Starbucks has also made excellent use of YouTube. It encourages users to upload videos not only of Starbucks TV commercials but also educational videos about the origins of coffee and the charitable work undertaken by Starbucks.

Recently, one of the most successful campaigns on Facebook was conducted by Budweiser during the World Cup soccer tournament in South Africa in 2010. The company launched its "Bud United Show Your True Colors" campaign on Facebook that enabled its followers to paint their faces virtually with the colors of their favorite team. The campaign generated a very high engagement level with an estimated 2.7 million people opting to paint their faces virtually. Nearly 1,000,000 people had clicked to "like" Budweiser's Bud United page by the end of the campaign. It was a classic instance of generating engagement with the company by using an interactive social media campaign.[14]

Nokia launched a Facebook campaign[15] that allowed users to click on the video to explore the features of its Ovi Maps, a navigational application on Nokia phones. The campaign resulted in more than 408 million impressions. Over 104,330 connections to Nokia's Facebook page were generated and 175,805 people watched the videos on Ovi Maps.

More important, the company was able to reach users in 12 countries within a very short span of time.

Mars was another company to successfully use Facebook to launch a new product. In the spring of 2010 Mars Chocolate launched M&M Pretzel.[16] Through Facebook the company was able to distribute 120,000 samples within 48 hours directly to consumers. In addition, the number of people connected to the company's home page increased by at least 9%, and the company had more than 1.2 million followers at the end of the campaign.

Although not many smaller companies have ventured into social media marketing, some have indeed used it to their advantage. In 2008 a small Sri Lanka-based company called Go Nuts with Donuts successfully advertised on Facebook[17] and with increased sales volume managed to open seven additional stores. The company currently has nearly 10,000 followers and regularly offers sales promotions through Facebook.

Entertainment companies have also made good use of the reach that Facebook provides to promote movies and theater productions. For example in February 2010 Sony Pictures publicized the movie *Dear John*; more than 1 million people connected to the *Dear John* Facebook page.[18] A Nielsen study found that the Facebook campaign was responsible for a 16% increase in overall audience awareness of the film. It also found that the campaign directly led to a 2% increase in "purchase consideration" for the film. Encouraged by the success of the *Dear John* campaign, Sony has actively started using the polling features available on Facebook to gauge audience interest in upcoming titles.

Similarly, 20th Century Fox has tapped into the word-of-mouth publicity generated on Facebook to publicize its movies.[19] Fox launched a highly visible campaign on Facebook to publicize the movie *Wall Street 2* a month before its release in September 2010. Twenty-six percent of people interviewed in an exit poll after seeing *Wall Street 2* reported seeing advertising for the movie on Facebook. A tracking study also found that more than 1.1 million people on Facebook were persuaded to see the movie after being exposed to the ads.

Twitter, unlike Facebook, does not have a self-serve ad platform. As such it imposes some limitation as to what brands can do in terms of direct marketing. However, Twitter has also been host to a number of successful marketing initiatives.

JetBlue was one of the major brands to join Twitter in 2007. Currently the company has over 1.6 million followers and extensively tweets to disseminate important information as well as obtaining feedback from users of the airline. The company claims that the response to its Twitter initiative has been outstanding and that Twitter has enabled it to communicate directly with its customer base almost instantaneously. The company solicits feedback on proposed route changes and benefits from getting the customer's perspective even on short notice. The airline company claims that their social media interaction has had a salutary impact on its image as a customer-friendly organization.[20]

Best Buy is another company that has successfully used Twitter to respond to customer queries. As of April 1, 2011 the company's *@twelpforce* Twitter account has provided over 45,000 answers to customer inquiries. More than 2,900 employees have also signed up to answer customer queries. According to the company the direct employee–customer interaction via Twitter has been a source of significant customer satisfaction.[21]

Comcast's innovative use of Twitter as a means to resolve customer grievances is noteworthy. Comcast's Frank Eliason discovered that by doing a search for the word "Comcast" he could find tweets that mention service complaints relating to his company. Using this innovative approach the company has addressed literally thousands of service complaints.[22]

With nearly 2 million followers on Twitter, Whole Foods has successfully utilized the social media site to engage with its customers. The company has used Twitter primarily as a customer service tool and responds to people who have questions about product availability at different stores, holiday hours, dietary information, and the like. It also provides links to the company's blog which has editorial content as well. An innovative aspect of Whole Food's Twitter initiative is setting up "niche" accounts such as having an account for cheese, @WFMcheese, or an account for wine, @WFMwine. This has enabled it to target niche customers of these categories.[23]

Dell was one of the first companies to openly disclose that it had made money using its social media initiative. In June 2009, Dell Computer announced that it had earned more than $3 million from Twitter followers who clicked through its posts to its websites to make purchases. Dell has half a million fans on Facebook and 1.5 million followers on Twitter. Dell distributes discount coupons through these channels and uses proprietary software to track sales. Alongside the traditional Facebook content, Dell also offers its fans access to their *Tag Team* app. It drives consumer engagement positively by enabling consumers to read and write reviews, buy Dell's products, and promote the brand by recommending it to others on Twitter and Facebook.

Mention must also be made of the marketing research usefulness of social media sites such as Second Life. For example, the First Opinions Panel in Second Life is managed by Market Tools which is a joint venture of Procter & Gamble and General Mills. The panel has more than 13,000 members and involves Second Life members who own the most virtual land, spend and earn the most money there, run the most groups, and spend the most time (averaging about two hours a day). The company hosts several Second Life Research Panels where they conduct surveys and interviews, focus groups, and the like. The company also collects observational data and conducts product concept tests, advertising pretests etc., within Second Life. Obviously, the superiority of researching in a virtual environment like Second Life lies in the fact that "researchers are able to view, measure and to some extent influence the peer interaction for decision-making that is not possible through web-based surveys." (Business Communicators in Virtuality, 2007)[24]

FUTURE TRENDS IN SOCIAL MEDIA MARKETING

The diverse nature of social media platforms has given rise to a large variety of highly creative and innovative strategies. Some businesses have used these networks largely to address customer complaints, and others have used them as channels to promote sales.

Lee Dung-Hun (2010)[25] performed a study on social media and identified four distinct trends. First, social media networks are fast becoming the preferred channel for customer care. Thanks to its reach and immediacy, customer concerns can now be addressed in a highly effective manner. If this trend continues, then they have the potential to supplant traditional phone-based call centers.

Second, social media can be used as a direct sales channel. Dell, for example, has linked Dell Outlet (where it sells refurbished computers) to its Facebook and Twitter accounts. Price alerts sent through these social media links generate traffic and sales at the Dell Outlet site. Encouraged by the success of Dell's initiative other companies including Lenovo have followed suit. Direct selling saves the company from having to go through intermediaries and will therefore be increasingly popular in the future.

Third, social media acts as an amplifier of word-of-mouth publicity. It is able to disseminate information to a very large segment of the population, directly and instantaneously. Furthermore, organizations can capitalize on social referencing to effectively communicate with their target customers. Businesses will increasingly seek to harness this capacity to create brand buzz and influence purchase behavior by the target audience.

Finally, the impressive success of deal-of-the-day sites such as Groupon, LivingSocial, and Woot will encourage others to emulate their examples and use social media as a platform for social commerce. For example, in January 2011 LivingSocial sold an amazing 1.4 million Amazon gift cards (for a total value of $14 million) within a single day; that's equivalent to 80 vouchers per second, 100,000 per hour, and $13 million in revenue. Earlier in August 2010, Groupon had sold 445,000 vouchers for the retailer, Gap, bringing in $11 million in revenue in the company's first-ever nationwide promotion.

From our brief overview of social media marketing, it is apparent that in the past two years there has been a dramatic shift toward user-driven social media sites. Traditional modes of marketing with their emphasis on controlled communication by professionals is fast being replaced by online user content and users' opinion. These developments have far-reaching consequences for marketing professionals. The empowerment of consumers makes it necessary for companies not only to listen but also to be proactive. The shift to listening and conversing through social media provides opportunity for marketers to craft their persuasive message creatively. Organizations can ignore the possibilities offered by social media networks at their own peril. However, getting in is easy but being successful in the social media realm requires a significant amount of planning and effort. Unlike traditional media, it will not suffice to merely increase spending on ads. Instead, a proper appreciation of the medium and how it can be tailored to fit the requirement of the organization is needed. A sincere and caring relationship with the customer base has to be developed. Social media are the highway to the future and organizations need to devise appropriate strategies to successfully navigate it.

ENDNOTES

1. Norman, J. (2010, November) Boomers Joining Social Media at Record Rate http://tinyurl.com/2wcmute.
2. ComScore 2010 US Digital Year in Review (2011, February) http://tinyurl.com/3g5ydbb
3. Age distribution on Social media sites (2010, February) http://tinyurl.com/yctss8r
4. Facebook Drives US Social Network Ad Spending Past $3 Billion in 2011 (2011, January) http://tinyurl.com/67hljag
5. Rawaski, K. Oreo Facebook Fan Page Example in Detail (2011, January) http://tinyurl.com/3bvhc5j
6. Society of Digital Agencies (SoDA) 2011 Digital Marketing Outlook (2011, March) http://tinyurl.com/3d9cyws
7. The Fortune 500 and Social Media, University of Massachusetts Dartmouth Center for Marketing Research (2010) http://www.umassd.edu/cmr/
8. Stelzner, M. Social Media Marketing Industry Report (2010, April) http://tinyurl.com/y2qdrag
9. McCracken, G. How Ford Got Social Marketing (2010, January) http://tinyurl.com/ydyhsrf
10. http://www.forrester.com/Groundswell/supporting/syncmyride.html
11. Wong, E. Clorox Collects 'Green Footprints' on Facebook (2010, Oct) http://tinyurl.com/2bbbmox
12. http://ads.ak.facebook.com/ads/FacebookAds/Bob_Evans_CaseStudy.pdf
13. Noff, A. The Starbucks Formula for Social Media Success (2010, Nov) http://tinyurl.com/yhj2hxe
14. 2010 World Cup Inspires Creativity in Social Media (2010, July) http://tinyurl.com/2a5bgq6
15. http://tinyurl.com/3mj6ylq
16. Olson, E. A Campaign for M&Ms with a Salty Center? Sweet (2010, June) http://tinyurl.com/2fava3d
17. ads.ak.facebook.com/ads/FacebookAds/Gonuts_CaseStudy.pdf
18. http://www.casestudiesonline.com/dearjohn
19. http://tinyurl.com/3wxv8m2
20. Case Study in Social Media Jet Blue (2008, December) http://tinyurl.com/6747tz
21. http://business.twitter.com/optimize/case-studies/best-buy
22. http://tinyurl.com/376lpa8
23. Second Life Market Research Panel Licensed to P&G http://tinyurl.com/y9nte49
24 Business Communicators in Virtuality (2007) http://tinyurl.com/2qt3go
25. Dong-Hun, Lee (2010, Oct) Growing Popularity of Social Media and Business Strategy http://tinyurl.com/3fbc8op

In order to better understand the strategic effects of social networking and building community, former eBay software engineer and risk analyst Matt North describes the online auction company's their ebbs and flows on their journey in building community through social networking.

Case Study: Social Networking, Online Communities, and Strategic Corporate Growth: The Rise and Fall of eBay

Matthew North
Washington & Jefferson College

Years before MySpace and Facebook made the term "social networking" a household phrase, the online auction company eBay was laying groundwork for turning online social groups into a competitive business advantage. Pioneering such concepts as user-to-user feedback and peer-provided support, and employing and adapting tools such as threaded discussion boards, moderated chat rooms, and eventually, live user conferences, eBay focused its early attention more on online community building than on transaction volumes, revenues, or even infrastructure. Although increasing sales figures and state-of-the-art technology eventually solidified eBay's long-term success and established the company as the predominant name in online auctions, it was the organization's early efforts to build community, and in fact camaraderie, that enabled the company to weather the significant storms of server outages, software and hardware failures, policy snafus, identity theft and online fraud, and well-funded competitive efforts from the likes of Amazon.com,[1] Yahoo![2] and even a joint Microsoft/Dell auction effort called FairMarket.[3] It was only when eBay lost focus on its significant online community of members that the company eventually stumbled. This social network had formed a solid foundation and given the company an undeniable competitive advantage during its early years, but today the question for the e-commerce pioneer is whether a company that has grown so large can ever hope to return to the personal friendly feeling upon which its success was built.

Founder Pierre Omidyar first created eBay under the name AuctionWeb over the Labor Day weekend in 1995. He got the idea from his girlfriend (who later became his wife), who was an avid Pez dispenser collector and commented one day that trading collectibles online would open up a whole new market. Despite the mythology surrounding the Pez-related beginnings of eBay, the first item sold on the fledgling auction site was actually a broken laser pointer, sold by Omidyar himself.[4] By the end of 1997, Omidyar knew he had a legitimate business model, the company had been remarketed as eBay, and growth was exponential. In a small booklet, *For the People*, published by the company early in the year 2000, Omidyar tried to share his vision for the company, emphasizing the importance of community building for successful online commerce:

> Early on, I realized the importance of supporting a community on eBay. A member's experience wasn't dependent on their interaction with us, but more on how they interacted with one another. Because of the e-mails I received from members as part of these interactions, I was thrust into the role of communicating the values I believed in, and setting the tone for those interactions. That's actually where the core values came from—basic ideas about people treating each other fairly and equally, respecting individuality, believing that everyone has something to contribute, and trusting that an honest and open environment can bring out the best in people.[5]

So how did eBay first begin to realize Omidyar's vision of "supporting a community"? It started with simple tools, tools not so different from a Facebook wall or a MySpace page. As the company grew, Omidyar would often get e-mails from eBay users who were having trouble using the website, trying to settle a dispute with a buyer or seller, or simply could not remember their password. With emails piling up throughout the week, he decided that it would be more pleasant if he downloaded them onto his laptop and answered them while sitting under a tree in the park on a Sunday afternoon. This strategy worked for a few months, but soon his website's transaction volume (and the accompanying email volume) became too great for him to keep pace. Even after quitting his day job in early 1996, he was not able to answer each person's query personally.[6] He hired a few employees, moved the auction business out of his spare bedroom into a rented office space, and still the email volume grew.

Reflecting on his core values for the company and his vision of community, Omidyar created a series of threaded discussion boards, originally referred to as electronic bulletin boards, dedicated to the most common topics he'd found in his email: site usage issues, dispute resolution, new feature ideas, and so on.[7] These boards became sources for answers to frequently asked questions, and forums for individual eBay users to share their own experiences and expertise. Some people, primarily very active sellers on the site, became so involved on the boards that they were eventually offered employment as teleworkers for the company. Perhaps the most famous is "Griff," a Vermont native who wandered onto the site in the spring of 1996 looking for a computer part and essentially, never left.[8] By summer of that year, Griff was well known as a knowledgeable and helpful contributor, and before winter, he was officially recognized as employee number five, the company's first full-time customer support representative.

Griff was soon joined by other AuctionWeb aficionados who became paid teleworking employees. "Holly," "Sonny," "Lars," and "Anne" were among a dozen or so early site users who caught and shared Omidyar's vision for the company's online sense of communal support. These individuals formed the core of eBay's customer support department, and as support operations formalized and expanded rapidly between 1997 and the year 2000, they were called upon to instill the vision of community to hundreds of newly hired full-time support staff.[9]

Everyone at the company had a name, whether a pseudonym or their own, and each was taught not only the function of the business, but also the values and the importance of being part of the larger online community. eBay employees were eBay users, and those who came to the company with little or no experience using the site were quickly assimilated. In the language of corporate America, being "assimilated" might sound bad, perhaps downright frightening, but at eBay in the late 1990s, it was more like being swept up into a circle of friends. Those who were, by the turn of the new millennium, almost clamoring to work for the company actually *wanted* to be assimilated. By then, the term "eBay user" was no longer the norm, Omidyar's vision had never seen people as "users," "customers," or "clients"; if you used eBay, whether you were a company employee or not, you were a member of the community. A reference back to the previously cited quote from Omidyar confirms this: he refers in that statement to eBay users as "members" of the community he envisioned from the beginning.

Part of any successful community is the ability to express one's self to others in the group. Aside from being able to do this on the forums and in chat rooms, eBay introduced two additional tools in the late 1990s that aided members in expressing themselves online. The first, and arguably one of the most important, especially in the early days, was the Feedback Forum. Along the timeline of eBay features, this innovation was among the earliest.[10] Since the inception of AuctionWeb, members had wanted an opportunity to respond to one another and to share their person-to-person experiences. Various ideas had been shared, both within the company and on the discussion boards. Ultimately, the idea of feedback was chosen and implemented.[11] Although the actual function of feedback has been revised various times over the years, and has even become the source of some controversy,[12] the foundational role feedback played in shaping eBay's community cannot be disputed. A key element to building competitive advantage is trust. Customers, or in eBay's case, members, choose to participate with and patronize establishments that they trust. The feedback forum added a trust-measuring component to the user experience, and although there were some notable exceptions where a user with high feedback turned out to be dishonest,[13] in general strong feedback scores indicated a strong member of the community.

In addition to the feedback system, eBay also implemented a tool in 1998 that allows members to essentially create their own personalized web presence. This system, called *About Me*,[14] really has very little to do with the auction process, the core of eBay's business engine. *About Me* generates no revenue for the company, and actually costs the company money in terms of resources to support it. But *About Me* did something less tangible associated with the social networking aspect of eBay's success. It gave people a way to get to know one another. Rob Chesnut, who created eBay's Trust and Safety division, told the *Los Angeles Times* in 2007: "eBay doesn't have a product. We are in the trust business: making people feel comfortable doing business with someone they don't know."[15] Chesnut's comment illustrates exactly what *About Me* is all about: in order for eBay to succeed, there must be trust; and in order for there to be trust, people need to get to know one another. At a time when it was rare for eBay members to meet one another in person, *About Me* gave them a way to introduce themselves to each other.

Social networking aspects of the eBay experience grew and matured during the latter part of the 1990s and the first part of the 2000s, and the sheer size of the community began to pose a problem. eBay had firmly established itself as *the* place for online auctions, and one by one, competitors shifted their business models away from bidding or closed down their auction sites entirely.[16] Now eBay had a new sort of problem: how do you maintain a sense of community when the number of community members reaches into the tens of millions?

The tragic events of September 11th, 2001 presented an opportunity for a group of such magnitude to band together in unprecedented ways. In the wake of the terrorist attacks of that day in New York, Washington D.C., and Pennsylvania, a need for disaster relief was born. Unfortunately, this opportunity now stands as an example of a failed attempt at using an online medium to strengthen a community. Within just two days of the attacks, eBay announced *Auction for America*.[17] The program set what many felt was an audacious goal: Raise $100 million in 100 days to help the families of the victims of the tragedy. Employees in diverse departments—communications, marketing, engineering, customer support—came together to design, develop, support, and disseminate the program. *A4A*, as it became known, was hailed initially as "teamwork at its best,"[18] and received the endorsement of then-President George W. Bush.[19]

Although united at first, the community quickly began to divide into factions over *Auction for America*. At issue were a number of core complaints: charity auctions could only use eBay's own BillPoint payment service and not the more popular third-party PayPal; charity auctions enjoyed a short-lived preferential status as patriotic buyers chose these auctions over similar non-charity ones; eBay sellers of charity items had to cover shipping and optional insurance out of their own pockets; and perhaps most damning to the company, eBay seemed to be taking the lion's share of the credit while it was the buyers and sellers who provided the commercial activity to drive the charity, causing many to wonder: "What exactly were the company's true motives."[20] PayPal launched its own competing charity, Internet discussion forums lit up with harsh criticism of eBay, and the *Auction for America* effort eventually raised just one-tenth of its stated goal.[21] Rather than uniting the members, *A4A* had driven a wedge, one that contributed to the eventual demise of BillPoint and the company's reluctant buyout of PayPal.

As the nation began to heal in 2002, the company needed to recover from its own missteps and try to reinforce the sense of community that had become so integral to eBay's success. The company returned to its roots of online social media that brought members with common interests and common goals together. One of the first realizations of this objective came in the form of eBay University.[22] How better to help a growing community of users succeed than to provide a forum for them to learn how to engage one another, how to understand the rules, and how to maximize their efforts? eBay University offered forums for sellers to share their ideas and successes, gave instructions for buyers to avoid fraud, and provided a whole host of other user-oriented content as well. People joined eBay University together and went through the classes together, in much the same way traditional students unite on an actual campus. They began to get to know one another and to plan to work together. When specific issues arose, such as the acquisition of PayPal in the summer of 2002,[23] members enrolled in eBay University classes designed to teach them about integrating PayPal payment options into their auction business. Other hot-button issues such as endangered species or pet breeding auctions, which tended to stir up controversy, created opportunities for like-minded members to work together for a cause, and eBay University presented a venue for members to educate themselves on such subjects.

Shortly after the PayPal deal closed, another tremendously important event occurred in the history of eBay and its community of tens of millions of members. In June of 2002, the first eBay Live conference was held in Anaheim, California.[24] For the first time in a formal way, the community could meet face-to-face.

> "I didn't want it to end," said eBay member Cherbear. "It was like a family reunion." "It was an event whose time had come," said Tom Cotton, one of the coordinators of eBay Live. The idea for eBay Live was born out of a desire to really celebrate community, the buyers and sellers who are the heart and soul of this company. We've been amazingly successful working together in the "virtual" world, but we felt it was time. We wanted to bring the people who make up eBay, buyers, sellers and staff together face-to-face.[25]

The event was wildly successful; planners had hoped to reach 3,000 attendees, however, more than 5,600 eventually registered. But more important than the volume, members continued to build that centrally crucial sense of community:

We wanted to offer classes that would be useful for buyers and sellers of all experience levels. We wanted plenty of opportunities to really listen to our members and learn more about their businesses, what is working for them on eBay, and what their needs were.[26]

Panels of eBay executives and other staff hosted round table events. These sessions offered members a unique opportunity to get in-depth answers to questions about eBay policies, for instance, and allowed them to speak face-to-face with staff about how key issues affect their eBay experience.[27]

"Most companies are defined by their products, their executives, and their financial goals. Not eBay…eBay is defined by you [the members]."[28]

eBay Live became a staple for reinforcing member relations, and for having fun. Orlando's conference in 2003 featured a live performance by Weird Al Yankovic; in 2004 members reunited in New Orleans; and in 2005 the company welcomed the community to celebrate the company's 10 year anniversary with them in eBay's hometown of San José. A strong focus on listening to the members characterized these early person-to-person events. As 2004 gave way to 2005, it seemed that the company and its member community had reached the pinnacle of success. The stock price had never been higher,[29] nor had the number of registered users or the company's profits.[30] Having leveraged its own versions of social media and the concept of online community building in its meteoric rise to the top though, perhaps eBay suffered from a case of overconfidence, or simply lost track of the importance of those individuals who needed to trust one another, every day, for the concept to continue to work.

By the end of 2005, the tone and tenor of the dialogue between company and community had changed dramatically. Accusations, complaints, and criticism began to expose cracks in the company's once seemingly steel façade. Pressure from previous member frustrations with the company mounted. One example was the 2002 purchase of a $30 million corporate jet. In the midst of the storm of the "dot-bomb," as online retailers closed up shop around them on an almost daily basis, eBay spent extravagantly while community members lodged their concerns in the direction of what seemed like deaf ears. Rosalinda Baldwin, editor of the influential online auction newsletter, *The Auction Guild*, declared, "I think it's absolutely outrageous and ridiculous. It's obviously their decision on how they spend their money, but when they do their next price increase, people aren't going to be too happy knowing eBay just spent $30 million on a jet for Meg."[31] This quote illustrates clearly the change in tone and tenor: It's *their* decision how *they* spend. A sentiment of "us versus them" began to emerge. Rather than appease members, the company responded with relative indifference: "We find our executives spending more time in airport terminals. In the long, long haul, the cost of the jet will be what we would have spent having our execs fly around the world."[32] Busy with listing, selling, and shipping millions of items each month to make a few extra dollars or, for most full-time sellers, a middle-class income, a vision of corporate executives traveling the world in a private jet was not a very welcome justification. Still, the company's performance remained solid and membership and auction revenue grew, not just for eBay but for the members as well. In retrospect, perhaps a more sensitive response to this and similar incidents early on might have tempered the severity of the company's fortunes later.

At eBay Live 2006 in Las Vegas, the crowd was bigger than ever, more than 15,000 members came together, but their agenda was not to listen to Weird Al or trade colorful cards and pins, although certainly the company provided venues for such diversion. No, members were less interested in diversion, and more in being heard. Rather than dialogue and discussion between company brass and the lifeblood members of the site, conference sessions became downright confrontational. The company's stock price, which had reached its all-time pinnacle early in 2005, was in the midst of a precipitous drop from which it has still not recovered.[33] In addition, the company had very recently spent billions of dollars on a single transaction: the acquisition of Skype.[34] The price of the deal was staggering by itself, but what further flustered, even enraged, some members was that eBay could not seem to articulate what, if any, strategic advantage Skype would offer the core business platform. Dozens of side businesses that also did not seem to fit had recently been added, while the company raised fees repeatedly, and in essence, started acting a whole lot more like a business and a whole lot less like a community. Founder Omidyar, now married with a family, was spending more and more time at his houses in Paris or Las Vegas, on philanthropy, and on venture capital projects, and much less time evangelizing his early vision.[35] An almost incessant poaching of employees from companies such as American Express and FedEx infused a very different type of corporate culture, and the company hemorrhaged long-time employees, many of whom had grown rich on stock options and grants, but who had also embodied the community-focused version of the business.

Attendance at eBay Live dropped in 2007,[36] and again in 2008 where "the conference in Chicago was so contentious that a convention-center worker observing one session stated it was like attending a union meeting. The anger directed at managers and executives in that session reflected the general unrest among many of eBay's sellers due to the radical changes taking place in the marketplace."[37] Weighed down by the worldwide recession, eBay's stock price dropped below a split-adjusted $10, the lowest ever in the company's history,[38] even as other online giants such as Amazon[39] and Google[40] sustained growth. Finally admitting that Skype offered little benefit to eBay users and had constantly yielded a financial loss, the company divested the majority of their ownership in the product.[41] Ten-year veteran CEO Meg Whitman stepped down, stating: "It's time for eBay, and this community, to have a new leadership team, a new perspective, and a new vision."[42] Whitman was replaced by John Donahoe, an eBay insider, amidst a flurry of explanations for her departure:

> "Whitman wasn't as innovative as her counterparts at Amazon and elsewhere. They definitely need a bit of a change of direction. The biggest challenge is buyer activity. There's been buyer fatigue in the last year or so, with fewer people coming to the site and coming less often."[43]

In the years since Donahoe's appointment, little has worked to rebuild the sense of community and camaraderie upon which eBay built its success. A planned eBay Live event for 2009 was cancelled in the wake of the 2008 debacle in Chicago, and corporate communications and efforts to stimulate income have confused and alienated the core user base:

> "These days, even General Motors is included in eBay's new target market, and small sellers are wondering where exactly they fit in eBay's plans. [The company's communications] may have them wondering what's in store for them later this month when eBay announces its second set of marketplace changes that will [soon] go into effect."[44]

Recent additional changes to the feedback system have left users further disillusioned.[45]

A series of smaller, customer-focused seminars was announced for 2010 by Lorrie Norrington, who became president of eBay Marketplaces upon Donahoe's appointment as CEO. The intent, according to Norrington, is to "bring eBay fun, learning and networking to cities around the country."[46] Response to the meetings has been mixed,[47] however, the move, at the very least, signals an understanding that in a business model like eBay's, community matters. Many questions remain before there can be a resurgence of the type of collaboration eBay enjoyed in the early years. Is it actually possible to have a "community" made up of hundreds of millions of users? With so many differing value sets and opinions, can there be actual camaraderie and mutual support? Could any leadership team, regardless of how talented, ever hope to restore Omidyar's vision to a company that has grown so large so quickly? eBay today remains viable and profitable, so perhaps the biggest question of all is: was the loss of a close and cooperative online community identity in exchange for corporate growth and success worth it?

ENDNOTES

1. See http://glinden.blogspot.com/2006/04/early-amazon-auctions.html
2. See http://techcrunch.com/2007/05/09/yahoo-shutting-down-auctions-second-service-to-deadpool-this-month/
3. See http://www.microsoft.com/presspass/press/2000/Feb00/FairMarketPR.mspx
4. See http://www.ebayinc.com/history
5. For the People. eBay Corporate booklet. 2000.
6. See http://www.biography.com/articles/Pierre-Omidyar-9542205
7. See http://hub.ebay.com/community
8. See http://members.ebay.com/ws/eBayISAPI.dll?ViewUserPage&userid=griff%40ebay.com
9. See http://www.internetnews.com/ec-news/article.php/112831/eBay-Picks-Salt-Lake-City-for-Customer-Support-Center.htm
10. See http://pages.ebay.com.au/education/learn-to-buy-feedback.html
11. See http://pages.ebay.com/help/feedback/allaboutfeedback.html
12. See http://arstechnica.com/old/content/2008/02/ebays-new-feedback-policy-no-real-feedback.ars
13. See http://reviews.ebay.com/Feedback-Padding-Spoofing-by-Crooks-Frauds-and-Scammers_W0QQugidZ10000000001815707
14. See http://pages.ebay.com/help/account/about-me.html
15. See http://articles.latimes.com/2007/dec/26/business/fi-ebay26
16. See http://www.auctionbytes.com/cab/abn/y07/m01/i31/s01
17. See http://www.internetnews.com/ec-news/article.php/886251/eBay-Launches-Auction-for-America.htm
18. See http://academicearth.org/lectures/auction-for-america-teamwork-at-its-best
19. See http://www.gothamgazette.com/rebuilding_nyc/at_a_glance.shtml
20. See http://www.macnewsworld.com/story/13608.html
21. See http://files.shareholder.com/downloads/ebay/0x0x40190/5817cc3d-dd16-466b-b588-a1b827539f15/68733.pdf
22. See http://pages.ebay.com/sellerinformation/howtosell/university.html

23. See http://news.cnet.com/2100-1017-941964.html
24. See http://pages.ebay.com/community/chatter/2003Mar/eblive.html
25. Ibid. Tom Cotton.
26. Ibid. Tom Cotton.
27. Ibid. Daphne.
28. Ibid. Meg Whitman.
29. See http://finance.yahoo.com/echarts?s=EBAY+Interactive#chart1:symbol=ebay;range=my;indicator=volume;charttype=line;crosshair=on;ohlcvalues=0;logscale=on;source=undefined
30. See http://investor.ebay.com/annuals.cfm
31. See http://news.cnet.com/eBay-buys-its-own-friendly-skies/2100-1017_3-945670.html
32. Ibid. Kevin Pursglove.
33. See Endnote 29.
34. See http://www.pcworld.com/article/122516/ebay_buys_skype_for_26_billion.html
35. Viegas, Jennifer. (2007). *Pierre Omidyar: The Founder of eBay*. New York: Rosen, 83–85.
36. See http://internet128.com/index.php/2007/06/14/scenes-from-ebay-live-2007-in-boston-meg-whitman-seth-godin-and-more/
37. See http://blog.auctionbytes.com/cgi-bin/blog/blog.pl?/comments/2009/7/1247519813.html
38. See Endnote 29.
39. See http://www.guardian.co.uk/technology/2009/oct/23/amazon-profits
40. See http://www.wired.com/techbiz/it/news/2008/01/google_recession
41. See http://techcrunch.com/2009/09/01/confirmed-ebay-sells-skype/
42. See http://news.cnet.com/8301-10784_3-9856612-7.html
43. Ibid. Aaron Kessler.
44. See http://blog.auctionbytes.com/cgi-bin/blog/blog.pl?/comments/2009/7/1247519813.html
45. See Endnote 12.
46. See Endnote 40.
47. Ibid. See especially the 'Comments' section.

REFERENCES

Liebowitz, J. (2007), *Social Networking: The Essence of Innovation*, Scarecrow Press, Lanham, MD.

Liebowitz, J. (2010), Strategic Intelligence, Social Networking, and Knowledge Retention, *IEEE Computer*, February.

6

Gaining Competitive Advantage through Virtual Worlds

As we apply technologies in the future, organizations will continue to look at creative ways for providing training and professional development for their employees and marketing and sales of their products and services. An interesting approach that some organizations are already using involves virtual worlds. According to Wikipedia, a virtual world "is a genre of online community that often takes the form of a computer-based simulated environment, through which users can interact with one another and use and create objects" (http://en.wikipedia.org/wiki/Virtual_world). Virtual worlds involve interactive 3D virtual environments whereby avatars represent various individuals that interact within this virtual world. Various application domains have been used for virtual worlds including medical, social, educational, commerce, training, entertainment, and other applications. The Starlight Children's Foundation, for example, uses a virtual world environment to allow children with life-threatening diseases to interact and explore their understanding of their illness with others in a safe environment (http://en.wikipedia.org/wiki/Starlight_Children%27s_Foundation).

When organizations think of virtual worlds, typically Second Life (www.secondlife.com) is used as the interactive 3D virtual environment whereby users can create their avatars and environment for their application area. There is developed property already built for a virtual world application, and undeveloped land whereby users can create their own properties and environment, so to speak. Goodwill Industries, for example, was prototyping a Second Life application for the donation part of their business. Also, many organizations are using Second Life for training and education. For example, Second Life Work is the leader of compelling, cost-effective virtual education solutions to amplify an existing curriculum or create new models for engaged collaborative learning (http://wiki.secondlife.com/wiki/Second_Life_Education). At the University of Maryland University College, as discussed later, a Second Life application is used for educating our graduate students in aspects of information technologies.

According to a 2009 report from Forrester, only 11% of enterprises have used virtual world technology to augment their work (http://www.forrester.com/rb/Research/real_value_of_virtual_worlds/q/id/54478/t/2). However, even over the past two years, there seems to be some growing interest in the potential use of virtual worlds for business applications. As an example of this interest, the November 2011 Virtual Goods World Asia Conference focuses on the following (http://www.terrapinn.com/2011/virtual-goods-world-asia/):

- How to build your business model around virtual goods
- How major brands can benefit from the industry and increase their visibility
- How to monetize virtual goods and payment platforms
- How to run a virtual economy
- How to acquire new customers through focused strategies and marketing

Even the federal government is looking into the use of virtual world technology. The Federal Virtual Worlds Challenge 2011, through the U.S. Department of the Army, was established with monetary prizes to look at the world's best implementations of virtual world environments, (http://www.fvwc.army.mil/). Military and healthcare applications are the main government examples of virtual worlds.

VIRTUAL WORLDS: LOOKING AHEAD

In the coming years, training and education will continue to be a popular area for use of virtual world technologies. Immersing oneself in an interactive simulated environment to improve one's knowledge and skills further is a nonthreatening useful application for organizations to apply. In perusing the Second Life site (www.secondlife.com), there is a preponderance of applications in the training area. According to Montalbano (2010), the U.S. Army is planning a Second Life-like environment that will simulate military peacekeeping operations and act as a training ground for soldiers. Previously, in 2008, the U.S. Air Force developed MyBase, a simulated Air Force Base in Second Life (Montalbano, 2010).

For education, virtual world applications have been used in recent years. For example, Suffolk University in Boston has used virtual worlds, as follows (http://www.suffolk.edu/31346.html; October 14, 2008):

> And that's exactly what Michael Kraten, Assistant Professor of Accounting, is doing. He uses virtual reality (VR) to teach students in the Sawyer Business School, allowing them to sign on to classes from remote locations. His avatar delivers lectures, answers questions and motivates students to excel just as he does in real-life classes, thus easing the strain on campus facilities and limiting students' commuting time. ... Virtual reality offers other benefits as well. Last year, Kraten took an undergraduate class on a virtual tour of Avnet, a Fortune 500 technology company headquartered in Phoenix. He is planning additional corporate tours this year to virtual campuses, which resemble their brick and mortar counterparts. According to Kraten, virtual reality "is the most cost effective way of connecting the people of Suffolk with people around the world with a minimum of effort to accomplish our global mission."

Businesses will also apply virtual worlds technology for their training and professional development of their employees, as well as for marketing and sales. Already, organizations are using virtual worlds for medical training and emergency preparedness training. According to Tasner (2010), "Marketing using virtual reality worlds and methods is one of the more advanced Web 3.0 tactics that you can use to generate leads, close business, even to communicate with your team." Also, with the new generation being adept in social media and mobile computing, they are also quite familiar with virtual worlds. Thus, businesses may increasingly market to this community with virtual world and related technologies.

The next section demonstrates how industry, government, and universities are gaining value from using virtual world technologies, especially through Second Life.

Case Examples: Competitive Advantage Through Virtual Worlds

Irena Bojanova
University of Maryland University College

Organizations with distributed teams and distributed users are increasingly common in the new era of globalization and information technology. They may gain competitive advantage utilizing virtual worlds for training, corporate events, and brand management. An important characteristic of virtual environments is that they add the feel of physical presence: participating as avatars, the learners/employees/consumers can feel to a large degree as if virtual collaboration and virtual products are real.

Many organizations have been utilizing Second Life (http://secondlife.com) to gain competitive advantage, as it is the fastest growing avatar-based virtual world and a promising media channel for collaborative teamwork, marketing, and advertising. For example, IBM, Northrop Grumman, Cigna, Intel, and Wells Fargo are using Second Life for training, corporate events, and trade shows. After creating their avatars, the users of Second Life can gather in the virtual environment and speak via microphones, chat through text messages, share documents, watch presentations, and participate in virtual simulations. The creator of Second Life, Linden Research Inc., is planning to add features for calling into virtual meetings from landlines or mobile phones, and is testing hardware that will allow companies to create private virtual venues.

TRAINING AND TEAM-BUILDING

Virtual training (v-training) is one of the ways organizations are gaining competitive advantage through virtual worlds. Currently, there are over 700 academic/training institutions in Second Life, actively proving that it is a promising virtual platform for supporting collaborative online learning. As avatars, the learners can participate in virtual lectures, simulations, and interactive skills development activities, and conduct virtual presentations. For example, Northrop Grumman. developed and created in Second Life a military contractor's secure Space Park installation, where American soldiers and police officers from across the United States can spend hours training on how to operate the Cutlass bomb disposal robot.[1] Conveniently, as Space Park exists only in cyberspace, the soldiers and police officers are able to participate from their different geographical locations without the need to drive or fly to get there.

As another example, graduate students from the Information Technology Systems (ITS) department at the University of Maryland University College (UMUC) periodically go on virtual educational tours in Second Life.[2] Military, government, and private companies' employees, who are working toward their ITS graduate degrees, are able to learn through virtual simulations and demonstrations about computer, mainframe, and server architectures, and about the evolution of data centers. Very useful venues for such explorations in Second Life are the Dell City–Dell Island, the IBM Systems EduCenter Island, and the Sun Microsystems Public Sim Island. Other intriguing tour locations are the U.S. Department of Energy's (DOE) Island, the U.S. Military Veterans Center, the U.S. National Oceanic and Atmospheric Administration (NOAA) Island, and the Siemens Innovation Connection Center. To provide details on a few: At the IBM Server Tower, students can watch educational sessions about the System Z10 mainframe, the Power 595 processor, and the IBM blade server center. The interactive environment allows each participant to open the mainframe computer doors and explore its parts. At the IBM BladeCenter Serviceability Pavilion, through virtual simulations, students can learn how to add a blade and how to replace a faulty memory in a blade server. At the Sun Island, students can be introduced to the Evolving Data Center and the challenges in migrating from a legacy data center to one built on future technologies. At the U.S. DOE Island, students can look at the variety of DOE informational resources, smash into their friends as subatomic particles, and take a tour of a supercollider. At the U.S. Military Veterans Center and the U.S. NOAA Island, students can have fun through virtual skydiving and weather balloon riding experiences.

Conducted surveys clearly indicate that the students have a positive and rich experience during the virtual educational tours. They find the activities to be engaging and interactive (92.7%), collaborative (85.4%), academically challenging (70%), instilling a sense of curiosity and discovery (94.5%), and provoking critical thinking (83.7%). The students strongly agreed that the tours are a fun experience (87.3%) and that they want similar activities in other classes (72.7%). The results indicate that through the virtual educational tours both key pedagogical goals and student satisfaction are attained, a combination difficult to achieve for any classroom activity. The demographics of the surveyed students is as follows: 73.6% male; 71.7% with average technical skills, 83% employed full time; 13.2% in the 16–25 age range, 34% in the 26–35 age range, 32.1% in the 36–45 age range, 17% in the 46–55 age range, and 3.8% in the 56–65 age range.

Team-building activities are another way for organizations to gain competitive advantage through virtual worlds. A big challenge for distributed teams is the lack of face-to-face interaction, ad hoc discussions in the hallways, and team building that rely on rapport development. Face-to-face gatherings, which help teams build trust, are rare and often cost-prohibitive for distributed teams. However, virtual worlds offer an affordable alternative for team development, providing direct communication, feel of physical presence, emotional engagement, and social interaction. As an example, using principles derived from social psychological theory, the IBM Social Computing Group designed and created in Second Life a collection of three team-building games: Crossing the Ravine, Tower of Babble, and Castle Builder. The games allow distributed teams to reflect on their work practice and help team members develop deeper ties at a distance.[3] Each game requires all team members to participate, as it is almost impossible to find a solution if the team does not work together and does not communicate efficiently.

In Crossing the Ravine, a team of five encounters a ravine that can be passed only through a bridge formed by properly connecting the objects that the team members possess. Tower of Babble is a stacking game, whose goal is to balance as many differently shaped blocks on top of each other without falling over. The team aims to get maximum points for both the height of the tower and the value assigned to each placed block. The last game requires designing and building a castle out of a set of pieces. The castle has to be designed by one team and built by another team; the builders cannot view the design and must rely only on information communicated by the designers; the designers cannot manipulate the castle pieces. The built castle is scored for originality, difficulty, and faithfulness to the design.

The IBM game developers discovered that Second Life provides "a remarkable social sandbox;"[3] while building the games they had situations when other avatars spontaneously provided feedback, helped with ideas, and tested the games. They also realized that there is no need to schedule meetings for feedback, as the games were on display at all times and anybody could test and provide feedback without solicitation. The developers found out that the games enable role formation, cooperation, and communication between team members, and elicit social behaviors from participants when they succeed, such as group celebrations and spontaneous dancing.

As another example, because academia has to emphasize on developing virtual teamwork and leadership skills, the Information Technology Systems (ITS) department at UMUC has implemented an immersive group project practice for one of its core IT courses that allows conducting effective collaborative research on dynamic virtual demonstrations and simulations related to course objectives.[4] The approach focuses on developing virtual team-building through engaging, but goal-oriented, simulation games and scavenger hunts in Second Life: geographically dispersed instructors and student-teams work across boundaries, conducting avatar-based meetings, team-building exercises, and group project presentations. The instructors and the teams utilize the virtual world as an enhancement to the standard online class environment. The approach has been applied to 10 ITS sections in Fall 2010, Spring 2011, and Fall 2011. The preliminary surveys show a very high level of student engagement and satisfaction from group assignments. The team-building exercises and the presented group work show high-quality teamwork and leadership-related skills development. The student teams show increased engagement, satisfaction, and online group work quality.

Preparation for the activities includes creation of Second Life avatars and location-based team formation. Once the teams are created, the members meet at a scheduled time in Second Life to introduce themselves and to decide on who to record the sessions and who to be a timekeeper. The team-building games (see Figure 6.1) are either goal-oriented simulations, based on collaborative work of at least three participants (such as Labyrinth), or brainstorming activities, based on reaching consensus without compromising (such as Survival). Each team-building game or scavenger hunt is scheduled for 30 minutes. The teams retrieve detailed instructions from predesigned notecard objects in Second Life. The scavenger hunt locations and milestones are carefully selected to complement the course objectives and material. Each team is advised to complete the activities in a timely manner, as they actually compete with all the ITS teams. The students take frequent snapshots and record the most interesting parts of their activities.

FIGURE 6.1
Team-building activities in Second Life.

Teams may decide to split during a scavenger hunt, however, all team members have to gather and take a snapshot at each milestone.

One of the goal-oriented simulations utilized for this approach is a Teamwork Tester from the Education Island,[5] which requires a ball to be moved by four team members over a curved path. Each participant may move the ball in only one direction: forward, back, right, or left. The team has to carefully coordinate how and when each team member should move the ball, so that altogether they properly guide the ball from start to finish. In case the ball gets too far away from the intended path, a siren sounds, the ball returns to the start position, and the team starts anew. In addition, the tester does not allow team members to communicate verbally. In this way, the player's attention and action correlation become even more important for mission success. Student creativity in this direction included flying over the tester field and communicating through gestures.

One example of a conducted scavenger hunt is as follows: (1) Locate the "Dell City–Dell Island" in Second Life. Go to the Travel Center and ride the tram over to the Giant Computer. Walk into the computer and locate the RAM chip. Gather the group and take a snapshot of all team members, sitting on the RAM chip. Then find the Circuit Board, gather the group there and take a snapshot. (2) Locate the Computer History Museum in Second Life. Locate the ILLIAC I computer and find out when it was retired. Gather the group and take a snapshot of all team members, staying in front of the computer. Note: It is up to the teams to decide how to split the work. However, it is important that all team members are present in the required snapshots.

The unique integration of virtual environments with traditional online learning management systems has proved to create a new rich and engaging platform for conducting virtual team-building activities that support team member interaction, reflection, and collaboration. Conducted surveys confirm definite improvement in student engagement and satisfaction, as well as in team building, presentation, and communication skills development. The students find that Second Life helps enhance collaboration (95.8%), know team members better (100%), feel physical presence (95.7%), and conduct final project presentations (87.5%). They also find that the virtual group project activities helped develop their communication skills (70.8%), team-building skills (83.3%), and technical skills (83.4%). Even before signing up for a project, conducted in Second Life, 93.7% of the students thought such a project would be more fulfilling and adventurous than a regular case-study project, although 57.9% of them were aware it would be more time consuming than a regular group project. The demographics of the surveyed students were as follows: 70% male; 62.5% with average technical skills, 83% employed full time; 8.3% in the 16–25 age range, 29.2% in the 26–35 age range, 33.3% in the 36–45 age range, 25% in the 46–55 age range, and 4.2% in the 56–65 age range.

CONFERENCES AND CORPORATE EVENTS

Virtual conferences hosted for employees or business partners are another way for organizations to gain competitive advantage through virtual worlds. For example, in July 2009, Cisco Inc. held the Cisco Live Conference both face-to-face in San Francisco and virtually in Second Life. This educational and training event for IT, networking, and communications professionals, gathered 10,000 attendees in real life and 3,000 more attendees in the virtual conference environment. The virtual video center offered keynotes and highlights, panel discussions on education in virtual worlds and on sensor networks, and experts' technical chats on wide area network services, products for the remote workforce, and secure unified communications. The participants were able to watch how data centers are evolving to deliver the architectural foundation for next-generation cloud computing architectures[6] and to amuse themselves at the gift center, picking up wizard hats and boxed gifts.

As another example, in October 2009, instead of scaling the event back because of the recession, IBM hosted its annual gathering of 250 leading thinkers in Second Life.[7] During the three-day event, participants attended 3 keynotes and 37 breakout sessions. Compared to a real-life event, with the virtual conference, IBM saved over $350,000; from that $250,000 was saved from travel and venue costs and $100,000 was additional productivity gains, as participants could continue working in their offices right after the event ended.

Virtual employee meetings, business meetings, and other corporate events that facilitate the building of relationships are one more way for organizations to gain competitive advantage through virtual worlds. For example, the IBM Global Innovation Outlook (GIO) team considers virtual worlds to be a great place to host very real-world, business-oriented roundtable discussions.[8] Their experience shows, meeting, collaborating, and brainstorming in a virtual world can be very creative. In January 2010, the GIO team facilitated a roundtable discussion on Smarter Cities with subtopics on public safety, transportation, education, social services, energy and utilities, and healthcare. During the virtual discussion, they were able to use unique, custom-made brainstorming tools such as a "BrainBoard" and an "Opinionator."

The BrainBoard—a virtual board with sticky notes—was utilized for introductions and during the roundtable discussion. The participants had to answer questions by putting a note on the board and then a facilitator organized the answers into sections. The Opinionator—a virtual area broken up into labeled sections—was utilized for participants to "vote with their feet," responding to questions as they walk into different virtual sections. This kind of interactive polling was found to be informative and entertaining. Through the virtual roundtable discussions, the GIO team was able to extend their relationships building on an existing IBM partnership.

MARKETING AND BRAND MANAGEMENT

Virtual commerce (v-commerce), as an interactive and immersive complement to electronic commerce (e-commerce), is yet another way for organizations to gain competitive advantage through virtual worlds. Successful marketing communication and brand management in virtual worlds is based on product databases and the use of spokes-avatars for vivid, immersive, multimodal social interactions.[9] A spokes-avatar serves as an organization or brand representative, a personal shopping assistant, or a recommendation and persuasion agent. In virtual malls and during trade shows, the consumers are able to view and explore the products, their packaging, and other features just as in a physical store or convention center. The virtual experience is positively influenced by the increased level of physical presence brought by the spokes-avatars.[10]

In a virtual world, organizations could research consumers' behavior and preferences more easily, as changes in virtual setups can be done instantly and at zero cost. For example, a company could explore whether altered configurations make a difference, monitor what the consumers like, or compare the traffic patterns in a store that is a replica of a real-world store. Realizing all these advantages, numerous organizations have embraced the idea of virtual commerce, marketing, and brand management. As a result, in 2009 alone, the total size of the Second Life economy grew 65% to U.S. $567 million, which is about 25% of the entire U.S. virtual goods market.[11]

ENDNOTES

1. Morrison, S. (August 2009). *Wall St. Journal*: A second chance for Second Life; Northrop, IBM use virtual world as setting for training, employee meetings. p. A27; http://www-03.ibm.com/ibm/academy/meeting/wsj_article_08192009.shtml
2. Bojanova, I. and Pang, L. (August 2010). Enhancing graduate courses through creative application of cutting edge technologies. *The Learner*, 17: 3, 225–240; http://irenabojanova.cgpublisher.com/product/pub.30/prod.2679
3. Ellis, J., Luther, K., Bessiere, K., and Kellogg, W. (2008). Games for virtual team building. *Proceedings of the 7th ACM conference on Designing Interactive Systems (DIS 2008)*. http://jellis.org/work/vw-dis2008.pdf
4. Bojanova, I. (November 2010). Immersive group projects for graduate information technology courses. *Proceedings of the17th Sloan-C International Conference on Online Learning;* http://sloanconsortium.org/2010aln/presentation/immersive-group-projects-graduate-information-technology-courses
5. Heiphetz, A. Training simulations and metrics in Second Life. Delta L Training; http://www.deltaltraining.com/SLWorkshop/Training_Simulations_and_Metrics_in_Second_Life2.pdf
6. Cisco. (2009). Data Center at Cisco Live 2009; http://www.cisco.com/web/learning/le21/le34/datacenterlive/index.html
7. Werner, T. (March 2009). Case study on an IBM Conference in Second Life; http://www.brandon-hall.com/workplacelearningtoday/?p=3638
8. Gandhi, S. (January 2010). IBM dives into Second Life – *Meeting, collaborating, and brainstorming in a virtual world*. *IBM developerWorks;* http://www.ibm.com/developerworks/opensource/library/os-social-secondlife/index.html?ca=drs-
9. Jin, S. and Sung, Y. (2010). The roles of spokes-avatars' personalities in brand communication in 3D virtual environments. *Journal of Brand Management*, 17: 317–327; http://www.palgrave-journals.com/bm/journal/v17/n5/abs/bm200918a.html

10. Jin, S. and Bolebruch, J. (2010). Virtual commerce (V-commerce) in Second Life: The roles of physical presence and brand-self connection. *Journal of Virtual Worlds*, 2:4; http://journals.tdl.org/jvwr/article/viewArticle/867
11. 2009 End of Year Second Life Economy Wrap up; http://community.secondlife.com/t5/Features/2009-End-of-Year-Second-Life-Economy-Wrap-up-including-Q4/ba-p/653078

REFERENCES

Montalbano, E. (2010). Army to develop virtual world for training, *InformationWeek*. June 8.
Tasner, M. (2010). Virtual Reality Worlds: The How's and Why's of this Unique Marketing Universe, *Huffington Post*, July 8; (http://www.huffingtonpost.com/michael-tasner/virtual-reality-worlds-th_b_638336.html

7

Gaining Competitive Advantage through Technology

In the foreseeable future, technology will continue to be an important part of the decision maker's toolkit. Organizations apply technologies to produce a competitive edge, and in the near term, the following technologies will certainly have an impact on organizations: cloud computing, mobile computing, social computing, search technologies, cybersecurity, and decision technologies.

CLOUD COMPUTING

According to Wikipedia, cloud computing is "location-independent computing, whereby shared servers provide resources, software, and data to computers and other devices on demand, as with the electricity grid" (http://en.wikipedia.org/wiki/Cloud_computing). Computing is done "in the cloud" which is a metaphor for the Internet. One key advantage of cloud computing is that organizations can generally save money as they can pay companies, such as Amazon, for storage and they only need to pay for the storage they use (http://www.associatedcontent.com/article/2052513/the_advantages_and_disadvantages_of.html). A limitation of cloud computing is security issues. However, with the attention that cloud computing is getting, such as being in President Obama's FY11 budget, appropriate models of cloud computing and related security measures should be addressed. Cloud providers including Microsoft, Amazon, Google, AT&T, and others are offering their services, and more and more companies are signing up (such as Netflix, British Telecom, *The New York Times*, Nasdaq, and others).

MOBILE COMPUTING

Another important technology trend that will continue to proliferate is mobile computing. Mobile phones/smart phones, tablets, and netbooks seem to be a natural part of the business environment. Over the coming year or two, there will be stiff competition among both hardware and software components in the mobile computing arena.

When we look at e-learning for education, training, and professional development, two trends seem quite apparent: mobile computing and personalization. We will see more development and use of incorporating e-learning through mobile devices and personalizing the education modules tailored for the individual user. The Center for Knowledge Management and Knowledge Technologies in Austria, for example, has been looking at personalization models for e-learning (http://know-center.tugraz.at).

SOCIAL COMPUTING

Along with mobile computing, there will be increased usage of social media computing. Already, Facebook has well over 600 million users worldwide, and in business, there is a proliferation of blogs, wikis, LinkedIn, Twitter, online communities, and other social media being used. According to Gartner, "business is getting social" (http://www.gartner.com/technology/research/business-gets-social/). The use of social media analysis to mine social networks can also offer new insights, as discussed previously in the analytics-related chapter. Social computing will continue to increase for product innovation and new product development.

SEARCH TECHNOLOGIES

Google has cornered the market on search technologies over the years, but it and other companies will continue to refine techniques to produce more tailored searches for the user. Semantic technologies will continue to develop to identify associations and concepts related to a query. Related to search technologies, e-book technologies will continue to play an important role in the years ahead. For example, Google's first acquisition of 2011 was eBook Technologies, which shows Google moving aggressively in the e-book space.

CYBERSECURITY

Computer security will always be on the minds of businesses. The more encompassing field of cybersecurity is growing at a rapid pace, and businesses are greatly concerned with possible cyberthreats, cybercrime, and cyberfraud. Unfortunately, in the United States, our supply of cybersecurity analysts does not meet the current and projected demand. In the Washington, DC area alone, there is a demand for about 30,000 cybersecurity analysts. At the University of Maryland University College (UMUC), new online masters and bachelors programs in cybersecurity technology and policy have been created with students entering this past fall 2010 (http://www.umuc.edu/programs/grad/csec/index.shtml).

DECISION TECHNOLOGIES

Decision technologies are advanced decision science related techniques that could help in the decision-making process. Examples include soft computing (such as fuzzy logic), multicriteria decision making, data/knowledge discovery, and other analytical techniques to help in structuring and evaluating problems. For example, the analytic hierarchy process (AHP), a form of multicriteria decision making, has been used over the years to quantify subjective judgments made in decision making. 3M, for example, has used it to streamline critical supply chain decisions (www.expertchoice.com). Soft computing, through fuzzy logic, has been used throughout the years to shed light on "uncrisp" reasoning. For example, some banks use fuzzy logic to streamline the approval process for mortgage loan decisions (Bojadziev and Bojadziev, 2007). Data and knowledge discovery techniques are being used to look for patterns and hidden relationships in unstructured data and text. Even the National Basketball Association is using these techniques for player evaluation and strategy (www.kdnuggets.com).

In order to better appreciate how technologies can affect organizations and the marketplace, Rhonda Chicone, vice president of engineering and product development at Notify Technology Corporation, discusses how senior leadership had to anticipate and react to the emerging technologies as Notify blossomed over the years.

Case Study: NotifySync™: No BlackBerry Enterprise Server™ Required!

Rhonda G. Chicone, Phd
Notify Technology Corporation

Notify Technology Corporation (www.notifycorp.com), an independent software company specializing in wireless solutions and services that provide secure synchronized e-mail, calendar, contacts, tasks, and notes access and management on a variety of wireless mobile devices and networks, was founded in 1994 by President and CEO Paul F. DePond. Headquartered in San José, California, the company was first created to develop computer telephony products such as voicemail notification and caller ID units for telecommunications companies. In 1998, Rhonda G. Chicone, then a senior software engineer, founded Notify Technology's research and development division located in Canfield, Ohio. Soon after, the company began conducting research and developing products for the wireless mobility market and moved away from the voicemail notification and caller ID market., Rhonda recruited talent from local colleges near Canfield, Ohio, and in mid-2001, Notify Technology Corporation launched its first wireless-based software system called the NotifyLink™ Enterprise Server. By 2011, Notify Technology Corporation had three commercially available software products: the NotifyLink Enterprise Server, NotifySync™, and NotifyMDM™. This case study traces the evolution of these leading products, especially NotifySync™, and describes how leaders can mesh current product technology and knowledge of industry needs to create new products that help maintain a competitive edge.

Four software engineers, and chief architect Rhonda, worked diligently in 2001 to launch the NotifyLink Enterprise Server. NotifyLink is a middleware software system that interfaces with Microsoft Exchange™ to gather users' e-mail, calendar, contacts, and tasks (PIM), and transfers the data securely to or from wireless mobile devices on various wireless networks. In 2001, there were only three major mobile device platforms and operating systems: Microsoft Windows Mobile™, Palm™, and BlackBerry™. For each mobile platform/operating system, there was a NotifyLink application that was installed onto mobile devices that enabled the NotifyLink server to communicate with it over the cellular networks, which did not have near the data transmission speeds as they did in 2011. However, in 2001 there were competitive obstacles as the NotifyLink Enterprise Server was not the only system on the market that concentrated on securely synchronizing information to and from mobile devices.

Research in Motion, the Canadian-based company that created the BlackBerry devices had a middleware software system called the BlackBerry Enterprise Server™. The BlackBerry Enterprise Server was tightly integrated into Microsoft Exchange and used Microsoft protocols such as the Messaging Application Programming Interface™ and the Exchange Administrator Software Development Kit™.

The architecture of NotifyLink was very different from that of the BlackBerry Enterprise Server because it was not tightly integrated with Microsoft Exchange. It did not use the Messaging Application Programming Interface or the Microsoft Exchange Administrator Software Development Kit. Instead, the administrator's interface was Web-based and the e-mail processing engine used the industry standard Internet message access protocol (IMAP4), which Microsoft Exchange supported. In fact, the PIM processing engine was the only part of the system specific to Microsoft Exchange. The architecture was designed to reach a broader audience by extending it over time to platforms other than Microsoft Exchange.

One of the main differences in functionality between the NotifyLink Enterprise Server and the BlackBerry Enterprise Server was that NotifyLink worked with both BlackBerry devices and other popular mobile devices such as Windows Mobile and Palm. The BlackBerry Enterprise Server, however, only worked with one kind of mobile device, the BlackBerry devices created by Research in Motion.

In the early 2000s, only professionals working at large companies had mobile devices. Many of the companies were satisfied with BlackBerry devices because they worked well for synchronizing e-mail and PIM; thus, during this period, the BlackBerry Enterprise Server was winning market share over the NotifyLink Enterprise Server. The NotifyLink

Enterprise Server was not penetrating the Microsoft Exchange market as Paul and Rhonda had originally hoped.

In 2001, Rhonda was promoted to vice president of engineering and product development at Notify Technology Corporation, and over the course of three years, a team of one became a team of 16, including software engineers, system test/quality assurance engineers, and technical support personnel. Frustrated with the failure of the NotifyLink Enterprise Server for Microsoft Exchange, Rhonda and Paul began to contemplate how to leverage the NotifyLink Enterprise Server in other markets because the product design had the potential to be easily changed. Paul conducted market research and determined that there was no enterprise class wireless e-mail and PIM synchronization software systems for Novell GroupWise™ that provided the robust functionality of the NotifyLink Enterprise Server. More important, at that time, there was no BlackBerry Enterprise Server for Novell GroupWise.

Novell GroupWise is an e-mail and collaboration system similar to Microsoft Exchange. Because of the NotifyLink Enterprise Server's architecture, the software engineering team was easily able to change the underlying foundation of the architecture to interface not only with Microsoft Exchange, but also with Novell GroupWise. The only part of the system that had to be re-engineered was the gathering of PIM. Therefore, at that time, Rhonda made the decision to redesign the system so it had a single PIM processor that could potentially interface with any e-mail collaboration system.

In 2002, more systems like NotifyLink Enterprise Server began coming onto the market. Even though Novell preferred NotifyLink, Notify Technology Corporation had to prove that their product met certain functionality requirements before Novell would endorse it. One requirement was to participate in a competition against systems similar to NotifyLink Enterprise Server. The competition was based on a set of requirements provided by Novell, who tested a total of five systems in their labs. Although this was a stressful time for the Notify Technology technical team, the NotifyLink Enterprise Server beat the competition and Novell endorsed NotifyLink in its various newsletters for their customers. Consequently, the NotifyLink Enterprise Server began gaining momentum in the Novell GroupWise market. Novell GroupWise customers started purchasing it because they needed a secure solution to transmit e-mail, calendar, contacts, and tasks to their BlackBerry devices, as well as to their Palm and Windows-based devices. However, although NotifyLink supported a variety of devices, BlackBerry devices remained the device of choice for most Novell GroupWise customers. NotifyLink for Novell GroupWise was not a failure.

Paul clearly understood that the NotifyLink Enterprise Server architecture could be easily extended to other e-mail collaboration platforms as Rhonda and the Notify Technology Corporation technical team demonstrated by creating NotifyLink, which interfaced with both Microsoft Exchange and Novell GroupWise. Paul charged himself with identifying all of the other e-mail collaboration systems that existed. He found many such systems and contacted the CEOs of each company. Every company that Paul contacted loved the idea of endorsing the NotifyLink Enterprise Server because their customers wanted BlackBerry device connectivity and most companies whose workers used mobile devices used BlackBerry devices. Moreover, Research in Motion did not have a BlackBerry Enterprise Server solution for the e-mail collaboration systems that Paul had identified. In 2002, this was very good news for the Notify Technology Corporation.

The NotifyLink Enterprise Server product evolved over the years, and by 2011, it interfaced with 13 different e-mail collaboration systems, including Microsoft Exchange, Novell GroupWise, Sun Messaging System™, Oracle OCS™, Oracle Beehive™, Scalix™, Zimbra™, Kerio™, MDaemon™, CommunigatePro™, Meeting Maker™, FirstClass™, and Mirapoint™. In addition, the NotifyLink Enterprise Server was offered to customers in two distinct ways. NotifyLink Enterprise Server On-Premise was an on-premise NotifyLink version that customers put directly onto their own server hardware behind their corporate firewall. The other was an on-demand version called NotifyLink Enterprise Server On-Demand™, which was Notify Technology Corporation's first software-as-a-service (SaaS), which implied it operated in the cloud. In addition, the NotifyLink Enterprise Server supported the latest and best mobile device platforms/operating systems, including BlackBerry, Windows Mobile 6™, Windows Phone 7™, HP webOS™, Google Android™, Nokia Symbian™, and iOS™ (iPhone, iPad, and iPod touch). Providing support for every popular mobile device used in the enterprise was very challenging for the technical teams at Notify Technology, but to compete, they had to meet the challenge and they did.

In June 2007, Apple changed the mobile device market forever by releasing the Apple iPhone™. At the same time that the iPhone came to market, so did the iPhone Software Development Kit™. The iPhone Software Development Kit was very limited in scope in that it did not have what was required to create an application for it that was able to transmit e-mail and PIM to and from the NotifyLink Enterprise Server securely as did other device platforms such as the BlackBerry devices. At Notify Technology Corporation, there was enormous pressure to develop a solution to the iPhone problem, otherwise the NotifyLink Enterprise Server would certainly start to lose market share. After extensive research, the technical teams at Notify Technology discovered that the iPhone used a somewhat unpopular protocol, at least at that time, created by Microsoft called ActiveSync™. In addition, Windows Mobile devices used ActiveSync to communicate to the Microsoft Exchange to receive e-mail and PIM securely; however, many companies were not using Windows Mobile devices because they still preferred BlackBerry devices and the BlackBerry Enterprise Server.

In response to the release of the iPhone, Rhonda and her team at Notify Technology Corporation decided to implement the Microsoft ActiveSync protocol for the NotifyLink Enterprise Server to support the iPhone. This approach was the only one that fit into the NotifyLink Enterprise Server architecture and could get to market quickly. However, because the protocol specification was not yet in the public domain, this was a very challenging task for the technical team. The Notify technical team used Microsoft Exchange, a Windows Mobile 6 mobile device, and a network-tracing tool to reverse-engineer the ActiveSync protocol. This approach enabled the technical team to analyze the ActiveSync protocol in an attempt to understand the protocol functionality, so that it could be implemented into the NotifyLink Enterprise Server. Once this was understood, the ActiveSync layer could then be implemented into the NotifyLink Enterprise Server to support the iPhone.

The first version of the NotifyLink Enterprise Server with iPhone support was released in July 2008; however, multiple problems quickly arose, many of which stemmed from the way that the ActiveSync protocol was implemented in the NotifyLink Enterprise Server. The main problem was that the ActiveSync protocol was new and Notify Technology Corporation did not have Microsoft's formal specification for it, but in addition, the iPhone had a whole set of its own problems. Interestingly, at the same time that Notify Technology Corporation was working to solve its iPhone support problems, so were many of the makers of e-mail collaboration systems, some of the same e-mail collaboration systems that NotifyLink supported. Because of its popularity, many providers of e-mail collaboration systems were also implementing ActiveSync within their systems to support the iPhone. This presented yet another problem for the Notify Technology Corporation with the potential loss of some NotifyLink Enterprise Server business. However, the lack of an ActiveSync application for BlackBerry devices turned out to be Notify Technology Corporation's saving grace. Many customers were not ready to accept the iPhone in their business environment and so the NotifyLink Enterprise Server continued to do well. Nevertheless, Rhonda and Paul knew it was just a matter of time before the iPhone was more widely accepted by the Enterprise.

Finally, in December 2008, Microsoft released the ActiveSync specification into the public domain. This was great news for Notify Technology Corporation because Rhonda and her technical team were then able to match the formal specification to their original reverse-engineered implementation and address all the related defects in the NotifyLink Enterprise Server. At that same time, Paul reached out to Microsoft and Notify Technology Corporation became an official licensee of the Microsoft ActiveSync protocol.

As Apple improved the iPhone operating system, it also introduced more security features making it more enterprise-ready. These improvements allowed companies and organizations to take a second look at the iPhone to determine if it had sufficient security and enterprise features for their employees to use it alongside a BlackBerry device on the BlackBerry Enterprise Server.

In addition, although it had been natively implemented on Microsoft Windows™ mobile devices well before the iPhone, the ActiveSync protocol was getting increasing recognition because it had been implemented on the popular iPhone. In addition, Microsoft steadily improved the ActiveSync protocol, which first started becoming popular in Microsoft Exchange 2003™. In 2011, Microsoft Exchange version 2010™ has the latest version of the ActiveSync protocol. Many companies and organizations had accepted both ActiveSync and iPhone in their environments, which required no middleware software such as the NotifyLink Enterprise Server or the BlackBerry Enterprise Server. In 2011, the BlackBerry Enterprise Server was still considered the gold standard for BlackBerry devices; however, ActiveSync and the iPhone (as well as the iPad™) became viable competitors within companies and organizations.

As the e-mail collaboration systems improved their ActiveSync implementations, organizations were starting to move away from the NotifyLinkEnterprise Server as a solution for the iPhone. Why suggest that their customers buy NotifyLink, a middleware system, when customers could connect their iPhones directly to their e-mail collaboration systems free of charge? Consequently, NotifyLink Enterprise Server sales began to drop. Paul and Rhonda felt that they had to address the problem by creating Notify Technology Corporation's next new product.

During a visit to Notify Technology's Ohio facilities, Paul and Rhonda sat down to brainstorm new product ideas, and in a matter of 20 minutes they had defined their new product. The new product was based on their premise and their experience interacting with their customers that companies and organizations still loved their BlackBerry devices, although the iPhone was certainly an option. They understood that people wanted choice. ActiveSync was becoming accepted at companies because of the improvements in the ActiveSync protocol, especially in mobile device security, and improvements to the iPhone itself. However, the only practical way to use a BlackBerry device successfully in an organization concerned about security was to use either the NotifyLink Enterprise Server or the BlackBerry Enterprise Server. However, both required a separate hardware server and middleware software. In addition, using the BlackBerry Enterprise Server required that BlackBerry devices had a BlackBerry Enterprise Server provisioning plan from their respective cellular wireless carriers. Paul and Rhonda's new product idea was to create an ActiveSync application for the BlackBerry in which the NotifyLink Enterprise Server or the BlackBerry Enterprise Server was not required and the end user would purchase a cheaper plan, called the BlackBerry Internet Service™ provisioning plan, from their respective cellular wireless carriers.

This new product made complete business sense because Rhonda knew she could leverage the existing BlackBerry software code base that the Notify technical team had created for the original NotifyLink Enterprise Server product. This coupled with the skill set and expertise about the ActiveSync protocol would make it easy for Rhonda to get the new product developed and to market quickly. The new product was named NotifySync™.

NotifySync software development began in July 2008, which was around the same time that support for the iPhone was released to the public for the NotifyLink Enterprise Server product. Knowledge transfer was crucial for the successful development of the NotifySync product. Rhonda created a NotifySync software development team and facilitated the knowledge transfer with the team that created the NotifyLink Enterprise Server ActiveSync interface. The knowledge transfer was successful, primarily because of the culture created by Rhonda at Notify Technology Corporation's Research and Development Center in Canfield, Ohio. The Center's culture was one in which communication, collaboration, and knowledge sharing was encouraged. No one worked as an island of knowledge, but rather shared knowledge.

After the NotifySync software engineering team worked with the NotifyLink software engineers to get a firm grasp of the ActiveSync protocol and how it was used in the NotifyLink Enterprise Server product, the software design for NotifySync began. The NotifySync product was launched to the public in November 2008. Both the NotifyLink Enterprise Server and NotifySync had to be revised when Microsoft released the ActiveSync protocol specification to the public in December 2008. This was not a problem for Notify Technology Corporation because they regularly improve their software products by releasing upgrades several times each year depending on the product; thus, both products were improved to meet the ActiveSync protocol specification.

NotifySync was a unique product in the market because users did not have to pay extra for a BlackBerry Enterprise Server provisioning plan from their wireless cellular carrier, but rather, the less expensive BlackBerry Internet Service provisioning plan was available. More important, NotifySync was a great option for those organizations whose end users wanted BlackBerry devices and had already accepted the ActiveSync protocol within their organization by using Microsoft Exchange but did not have a BlackBerry Enterprise Server in their environment. These organizations could deploy NotifySync to their end users because no BlackBerry Enterprise Server was required. The only items required were ones that they already had: an e-mail system that supported the ActiveSync protocol such as Microsoft Exchange (and many others) and BlackBerry devices or users who wanted to use BlackBerry devices.

That the BlackBerry Enterprise Server was not required was a significant development to an IT administrator, IT director, or CIO because there was now no need for additional hardware server(s) on which to place the BlackBerry Enterprise Server middleware software. In addition, it eliminated their need to manage and support the BlackBerry Enterprise Server system. These changes weighed heavily in a cost versus benefit analysis for companies, especially considering the economic climate in 2011.

Although Notify Technology Corporation had a direct sales team, shortly after the release of NotifySync, Paul approached Rhonda about the idea of developing an online store from which customers could purchase NotifySync. The primary impetus for the online store was to reach smaller companies and thus keep the direct sales team focused on larger organizations. An online store made perfect business sense and Rhonda's team built and launched the NotifySync eStore in May 2009. The eStore solved the problems for which it was intended. By 2011, NotifySync had remained a successful product for Notify Technology Corporation.

Interestingly, it was not directly planned but a pleasant surprise that NotifySync would also augment Notify Technology Corporation's next software product called NotifyMDM™. NotifyMDM was a mobile device management system intended to help organizations manage, monitor, secure, and support their mobile devices. The NotifyMDM system, like NotifyLink, was designed to work with all the latest mobile device platforms such as iOS, BlackBerry, Android, Windows Mobile, Windows Phone 7, HP webOS™, and Symbian. NotifyMDM was launched as a free trial on February 1, 2011 with the public release in April 2011. The advantage of NotifyMDM was that unlike other mobile device management makers that required a BlackBerry Enterprise Server to manage BlackBerry devices, NotifyMDM did not because NotifySync was available as an alternative. In sum a BlackBerry Enterprise Server was not required.

This case study reveals the importance of understanding four crucial factors that a software company's leadership staff should consider: first, is to analyze target market trends by finding the gaps and filling them; second, is to listen to what customers say to create new product development opportunities; third, is to understand how to leverage existing product technology to build new products to reach additional markets; and finally, the fourth item is to create a corporate culture of collaboration, communication, and shared knowledge to enable teams to move with agility to create new products. These four factors had major effects on Notify Technology Corporation's success.

REFERENCE

Bojadziev, G. and Bojadziev, M. (2007). *Fuzzy Logic for Business, Finance, and Management*, 2nd edition. Singapore: World Scientific.

8

Gaining Competitive Advantage through Human Capital

Most CEOs will say that their competitive edge is their people. It is hoped that their employees, or human capital, foster the creativity and innovation to allow their organizations to succeed. In some organizations, human capital takes a broader meaning by not only including the employees and management of the organization but also including the partners, third-party vendors, universities, contractors and subcontractors, consultants, and other entities that comprise the "human capital" of the organization. Because another chapter looks at "relationships," we focus here on the organization's employees and management as being the "human capital."

PEOPLE POWER

In the first chapter, we noted that knowledge management consists of various types of capital, human capital (the employee's knowledge and connections), structural capital (things that you cannot easily take home with you from the office such as intellectual property rights), social or relationship capital (knowledge from one's customers or clients), and competitor capital (the knowledge gleaned from one's competitors). Some organizations, like Sweden's Skandia, even quantify these various types of capital as part of their annual reporting process. Certainly, there is a strong link between human capital and knowledge management. For example, the recognition and reward structure is an important component for enabling the organization to build and nurture a knowledge-sharing culture. Figure 8.1 is an example of establishing certain levels of knowledge

Level 1	Knowledge Seeker	• Community member in organizational communities of practice (CoP)
		• Took the one-day Intro to KR&T (Knowledge Retention & Transfer) workshop
Level 2	Knowledge Sharer	• Active contributor and discussant on 1–2 CoPs
		• Serves as a member on KMWG (Knowledge Management Working Group) Subcommittee
		• Takes additional KM workshops (e.g., Kn. Audit, etc.) and attends KM conferences
Level 3	Knowledge Champion	• Leader/coleader of a KMWG subcommittee
		• Creates KM-related pilots
		• Gets new individuals in the organization to participate in KM activities
		• Educates others about the value of KM in a knowledge stewardship role in lunch and learn sessions
		• Presents at internal or external KM-related conferences/venues about the organization's KM effort

FIGURE 8.1

Three increasing levels of knowledge management engagement.

management engagement within the organization—going from a knowledge seeker to a knowledge champion.

These levels of engagement could be tied to the recognition and reward structure of the organization in order to promote knowledge-sharing among its employees. Also, more specific learning and knowledge-sharing proficiencies could be built within the annual performance review to both recognize and reward employees for exhibiting such behaviors. Table 8.1 is an example of possible learning and knowledge-sharing proficiencies.

KNOWLEDGE RETENTION ISSUES

In addition to knowledge transfer and recognition/reward issues, knowledge retention is another hot topic that will continue to be a factor in the years ahead as the baby boomers retire. Even though knowledge retention is a critical issue in such sectors as aerospace, manufacturing, energy, utilities, education, and others, many organizations still do not have a formal knowledge retention strategy. Government agencies (federal, state, and local) are also at great risk of knowledge loss due to the workforce demographics. From Liebowitz's research and the Institute for Corporate Productivity (www.i4cp.com), about 80% of the organizations surveyed do not have a knowledge retention strategy. This puts many organizations

TABLE 8.1

Knowledge Sharing Proficiencies/Competencies

Intradepartment Communications: Communicates well with those within his or her department

Interdepartment Communications: Communicates effectively with those in other departments

Knowledge Contribution: Shares knowledge through various knowledge management mechanisms, such as mentoring, conference trip reports, discussions via brown bag lunches, storytelling, lessons learned/best practice content contribution, online communities/threaded discussions, newsletter contributions, and so on

Collaboration: Actively participates in cross-functional teams

Knowledge Dissemination: Regularly distributes articles of interest to other employees

Knowledge Value: Shows value-added benefits from knowledge received from others and knowledge gained by others

Knowledge Creation: Willing to be innovative, take risks, and try new ideas

at great risk as critical knowledge may be lost by employees leaving the organization or moving to other parts.

In developing a knowledge retention strategy, Liebowitz (2009) indicates that there should be four components:

- Recognition and reward structure
- Bi-directional knowledge flow (top-down and bottom-up)
- Convenient codification and personalization knowledge management/knowledge retention techniques
- The Golden Gem: tapping the knowledge of retirees in creative ways

Various knowledge retention approaches can be used such as exit interviews, continuity books (do's and don'ts, frequently asked questions and responses, process flows, and persons/departments to contact), after-action reviews (what worked right, what worked wrong, how can we correct things for the next time), hot topic tutorials on selected topics, lessons learned/best practice systems, blogs, wikis, communities of practice, storytelling (organizational narratives), mentoring programs, emeriti and other retiree/alumni programs for involvement with current employees, job sharing, job rotation, and other knowledge retention techniques.

According to John Moore (2009), "[K]nowledge retention helps agencies retain employees' expertise." The Tennessee Valley Authority (TVA) has been actively involved in knowledge retention for many years. They use a variety of techniques from mentoring to Web 2.0 tools. Aerospace Corporation, Rolls Royce, Fluor, Jet Propulsion Laboratory, and a few other organizations have been cited by APQC (www.apqc.org) as leaders in knowledge retention. Even though there are some organizations that are leading the way, many organizations are far behind. Organizations should really start the knowledge retention process from day one of the employee's organizational life span versus waiting until two weeks before they retire to capture valuable knowledge.

Organizations should really have KR SOP (knowledge retention standard operating procedures). The nuclear energy industry in the United States is going through a resurgence from the 1970s through the 2010 New Reactor Program (U.S. Nuclear Regulatory Commission (NRC)). New nuclear power plant construction in the United States has been relatively dormant in recent years; much of the nuclear power plant construction and operations knowledge is "graying." Thus, there has been a strong push through the NRC, Nuclear Energy Institute, and the Institute of Nuclear Power Operations (INPO) to have workshops on knowledge retention and transfer and to develop knowledge retention and transfer SOPs.

WHAT'S AHEAD

Organizations should develop a human capital strategy whereby knowledge management should be one of the underlying pillars. Within that pillar, knowledge retention and transfer should reside. In the U.S. government, the OPM (Office of Personnel Management) strategic human capital framework for other government agencies includes six pillars, of which one is the "leadership and knowledge management" pillar (http://apps.opm.gov/humancapital/). The other pillars are: strategic alignment; workforce planning and deployment; results-oriented performance culture; talent; and accountability. In order to be successful, the chief people officer or chief human capital officer should spearhead this strategic human capital framework and work with appropriate executives, managers, and employees across the business units in the organization. The chief learning officer will also play an important role to be sure that continuous learning is incorporated within the organization's leadership and employee professional development programs.

The 2011 National Human Capital Summit, sponsored by the Human Capital Institute (http://www.hci.org/humancapital/summit-overview), focused on reactivating the workforce to meet the challenges of tomorrow. As organizations plan for their future human capital issues, change management will be an important element to consider and apply. Having the right change agents and change management processes in place will affect the success of an organization's human capital strategy and ultimate strategic goals of the organization. Competency management, performance management, knowledge management, and change management will continue to be essential elements in developing an organization's human capital strategy for succession planning and workforce development.

The next section discusses how PricewaterhouseCoopers has applied human capital and knowledge management strategies as part of their internal operations in order to gain a competitive edge.

Case Study: The Pursuit of Knowledge Management Maturity

Sloane Menkes and Denise Lee
Washington Federal Practice
PricewaterhouseCoopers

PricewaterhouseCoopers (PwC) is not only an audit firm; it is a place where innovators flourish. PwC was formed in 1998 from a merger between Price Waterhouse and Coopers & Lybrand and has a long history that dates back to the nineteenth century of serving clients with distinction. Both accounting firms originated in London during the mid-1800s. Today, PwC is the world's largest professional services firm and serves 26 industries in the fields of assurance, tax, human resources, transaction services, performance improvement, and crisis management. PwC is a recognized leader in knowledge management and was selected among the top 10 world's "Most Admired Knowledge Enterprises" in the 2010 Global MAKE study conducted by Teleos in association with the KNOW Network. A panel of Fortune 500 leaders selected PwC ahead of our competitors, cited for creating value based on its knowledge of clients and transforming enterprise knowledge into stakeholder value. This also earned PwC a place in the 2009 Global MAKE "Hall of Fame" as one of only 24 organizations to have been a finalist in each of the five past annual studies.

An example of innovative knowledge management in action at PwC is the Washington Federal Practice (WFP). WFP was formed in 2004 and is one of 17 business units within the U.S. firm of PwC. WFP delivers premier management consulting services to the U.S. federal government to enable government departments, their key programs, and their leadership to achieve transparency, accountability, and operational effectiveness. When PwC started this business unit, it did so with a vision to become the clear choice for providing management consulting to the federal government to promote managerial effectiveness. This was deemed an achievable vision given the firm's capabilities and brand, but it required a unique strategy aligned with disciplined operations to deliver consistent and valued quality. Within PwC, WFP is recognized as being in the top quartile of all the U.S. business units. PwC and WFP are highly ranked as role model organizations in areas that include best places to work, to have an internship, to receive training, for diversity, and in particular for knowledge management. For example, the WFP knowledge management team used a survey to document the return on investment (ROI) from use of the knowledge management system, tools, and services. The results demonstrated these factors have had a direct impact on winning over half of the total business revenue within a one-year period and supported the goal of pushing the knowledge management program to the next level of maturity. Throughout this case, some key leading practices used to develop the WFP knowledge management program and contribute to its success are outlined.

LEADING PRACTICE: CRITICAL SENIOR LEADERSHIP SUPPORT

The senior leaders of WFP committed personal actions over the past seven years that led the organization to phenomenal growth and achievement forming the basis of a growing business. These senior leaders are led by Scott McIntyre, a passionate supporter of KM. He infuses the practice with a high-performance, client-focused culture with a focus on excellence and sharing knowledge. WFP's client-based work is increasingly knowledge intensive and managing that knowledge is a key business driver and enabler. WFP's forward-thinking senior leaders understand this. A knowledge management program represents change, and change induces resistance. The backing of senior leadership helps overcome that resistance. Leaders play an important role in setting the tone and morale of the workforce. The 2009 Best Places to

Work rankings noted that, "For the fourth time in a row, the primary driver of job satisfaction in the organization is effective leadership." Leadership demonstrates through actions their value of knowledge transfer and development of the workforce.

A 2008 American Productivity and Quality Center (APQC) study, titled Retaining Today's Knowledge for Tomorrow's Workforce, supports that

> [S]torytelling is another powerful tool for knowledge transfer. Stories can supply context for organizational successes and lessons learned, and each story has the potential to personalize an issue by bringing it alive for listeners and readers. Stories are also an effective way to bridge generational gaps, communicate important information about an organization's culture, and help employees develop a sense of organizational identity. In addition, the storytelling format allows experts and their audiences to participate in bilateral discussions, which is a benefit that one-way communication formats—such as lectures—cannot provide.

PwC uses stories to transfer knowledge throughout our learning programs, messaging, and specifically in our senior leadership communications. The WFP leader is a great storyteller and often communicates to staff of various generations the practice through the use of story on his All Hands Calls or regular WFP Update newsletters.

LEADING PRACTICE: KM SITS ON THE SHOULDERS OF IT

WFP relies on PwC's technology infrastructure that supports its professionals in the field. This infrastructure provides them with knowledge and information needed for decision making and serving clients. PwC has a vast technology infrastructure that includes 24/7 PwC Technology Support including fully deployed phone, web-based and e-mail access support from technicians, self-help tools, guides, and on-site support to ensure constant connectivity to each other and critical information. WFP information resources and technology, including hardware and software, are designed, managed, and operated by PwC as a part of the global PwC infrastructure. Reliability, security, and user-friendliness are designed into the hardware and software selected for use and carefully maintained and updated to meet the high-level requirements of WFP and the workforce. The average knowledge workers today are exposed to advanced technical capabilities on their personal computers and expect cutting edge technology capabilities in the workplace, especially younger generations such as millennials and generation X. To provide the utmost access and reliability with the firm-issued laptops and other infrastructure, PwC strives to match the industry benchmark of 24/7 availability. Real-time critical information is pushed daily to all laptops. Security of our hardware and software is critical to WFP in order to protect the confidentiality of client data and WFP intellectual property. WFP conducts extensive training so that all users are competent and comfortable in working with the hardware and software provided to them. The user-friendliness of our systems is always in a state of continuous improvement. This infrastructure provides the foundation for the knowledge management program that requires an advanced IT infrastructure to flourish.

LEADING PRACTICE: DON'T JUST DRIVE BLIND, DEVELOP A KM STRATEGY SO YOU KNOW WHERE YOU ARE GOING

Information and knowledge are what PwC sells to its clients, but for the first two years of operation, WFP stored knowledge in disparate databases with no real strategic structure. Through evaluation and a focused KM program in 2005, PwC developed a strategy and implementation plan for a knowledge management organization, including the necessary infrastructure that immediately benefited WFP. Launched in October of 2006, the program collected all information from legacy systems, applications, and functions into a centralized portal, the Knowledge Gateway. This world-class knowledge repository and supporting KM program represents a $100 million investment that contains immense quantities of historical knowledge and information compiled from databases, websites, applications, and other KM systems. The knowledge management strategy enables WFP to collect and transfer workforce knowledge; transfer relevant knowledge to and from customers, suppliers, partners, and collaborators; rapidly identify, share, and implement best practices; and assemble and transfer relevant knowledge for use in the WFP's individualized knowledge strategy, known as the Knowledge Agenda.

LEADING PRACTICE: IDENTIFY BUSINESS PROCESSES WHERE YOU CAN EMBED KM ACTIVITIES

Identifying and capturing transactional knowledge into clear steps has led to less reliance on verbal exchange and greater likelihood that responsibilities can be assumed by someone beyond the current incumbent. WFP has supported the investment of time to collect and document operating practices, as part of a streamlined business processes effort, because it saved time and improved quality in the long run. The management and retention of knowledge is an integral part of how WFP operates. The transfer and documentation of transactional knowledge is a basic need, yet it is often overlooked. One of the core documents developed at the outset of the program was the governance structure. Knowledge is managed according to specific guidelines included in the WFP Redaction Guide. This Guide ensures that WFP complies with specific constraints to knowledge due to content standards and client requirements. The use of the Guide also helps guard the identity of a specific client; protect PwC's, WFP's, and others' copyrights; avoids publication of confidential and sensitive material; and assures that WFP receives necessary approvals. All knowledge submitted into the Knowledge Gateway is filtered and rated by the standards developed by the firm.

LEADING PRACTICE: KEEP YOUR CONTENT UP TO DATE

The knowledge management system that is a key differentiator is the Knowledge Gateway. WFP fully deploys this portal across WFP, and it undergoes continuous updates through the collection of knowledge "deposits," and the use of knowledge by the workforce "withdrawals." WFP quickly became recognized as the knowledge management leader within PwC due to processes put in place such as strict content management procedures. WFP applies a performance improvement system to keep data and information availability current. An annual evaluation of the quality of knowledge published is conducted through "quality audits." This annual evaluation systematically refines and enables innovation of the knowledge used by our workforce and business partners. These annual audits also evaluate the relevancy of our content in the firm's knowledge repository. To help maintain the relevancy of information and the knowledge strategy, WFP Learning and Knowledge Champions and all staff provide input throughout the year on out-of-date content in need of updates. At WFP, content management is everyone's responsibility.

LEADING PRACTICE: BUILD KNOWLEDGE-SHARING BEHAVIORS INTO PERFORMANCE MANAGEMENT SYSTEM

The goal within WFP is to develop and share truly distinctive knowledge and promote organizational learning. Every WFP employee has a performance goal to share knowledge through the Knowledge Gateway at least four times per year. Organizational leaders and subject matter specialists are required to contribute "Thought Leadership" that helps position WFP as the thought leader for the federal government in our key market and capability areas. PwC has four behaviors infused in all aspects of the firm, and WFP supplements them as identified in italics:

1. We invest in relationships *to build trust with our clients.*
2. We share and collaborate *to promote team success.*
3. We put ourselves in each other's shoes *to ensure empathy and teamwork.*
4. We enhance value *to distinguish WFP in a crowded market.*

Leadership consistently reinforces these behaviors and they design them into the firm's performance management system. The behaviors are the foundation for a knowledge-sharing culture and the promotion of organizational learning values.

LEADING PRACTICE: CONTINUOUS NETWORK ACCESS TO INFORMATION AND PEERS IS DEMANDED BY THE KNOWLEDGE WORKER

At WFP, all work is knowledge work and the foundation for providing quality service to clients and to effectively manage the performance of our internal operations and processes. Therefore, it is critical that all data are accurate, have integrity and reliability, are available in a timely manner, and are secure and confidential. WFP is a role model organization for selecting, gathering, analyzing, managing, and improving our data, information, and knowledge assets and managing our information technology. Through exceptional reporting and use of our knowledge assets, we are able to rapidly access data for organizational reviews to understand and improve our performance throughout the organization, as well as support new business and client service initiatives. At WFP, information accessibility and availability is critical to accomplishing our work, because information and knowledge are what we sell to clients. Each professional is personally provided leading-edge tools to connect to the infrastructure and access the vast knowledge management system. At WFP information accessibility and availability is the lifeblood of our professionals.

These systems and processes are systematic and fully deployed throughout WFP. Our systems are networked and completely available to all authorized users 24 hours a day, 7 days a week. Each professional is issued a BlackBerry to enable connectivity to each other and our knowledge repositories. The mobile device is an expected tool of the knowledge worker and the interest in mobile applications is just increasing.

LEADING PRACTICE: EXPLOIT THE SWEET SPOT BETWEEN KM AND LEARNING

The goal of the high-performing, learning-based enterprise is a strong connection between learning and knowledge. WFP's KM function provides and embeds knowledge into the business through collaboration with the learning function, nurturing growth and change for both functions and the practice at large, by helping adjust the culture to emerging conditions with expertise and dexterity. Drawing from a well of pertinent organizational sources, information can be pushed out to the learners who need it through the Knowledge Gateway. Real-world experience from subject matter specialists serve as a litmus test to ensure that missteps uncovered in past experience are not repeated, safeguarding against errors and pushing vetted learning and knowledge assets through WFP. This enables the right people to connect to each other and the right knowledge to address the client need at hand and complete the project.

Through our comprehensive Learning and Education System (L&E) onboarding program, all new hires receive online and classroom training on the Knowledge Gateway and policies and procedures. In addition, WFP professionals have ongoing training and supplemental information available through our learning and education system that enables a continuous learning loop. As knowledge gaps are identified, training is developed and then deployed. The L&E system is highly integrated with the Knowledge Gateway KM portal. All learning is shared with the organization through training, communication, and the Knowledge Gateway to contribute to organizational learning.

As a role-model system, clients are turning to WFP for our expertise in this area. In the last 18 months, WFP has delivered its knowledge management expertise and the ability to incorporate learning programs to a number of external clients, further demonstrating its successful operation.

LEADING PRACTICE: EMBED CONNECTORS
WHERE THE WORK IS DONE

In Malcolm Gladwell's book, *The Tipping Point: How Little Things Can Make a Big Difference*, he discusses the moment when an idea, trend, or behavior crosses a threshold and tips to then spread like wild-fire. This moment of epidemic change is led by individuals known as "connectors." WFP has sought to harness that connector energy and direct it toward institutionalizing knowledge-sharing behaviors into the "DNA" of the practice. WFP connectors are known as Learning and Knowledge Champions. Champions volunteer to take a leading role in the firm's KM program and to act as ongoing liaisons to the rest of WFP. Perhaps most important, the Learning and Knowledge Champions program puts a trusted coworker's familiar face onto a KM initiative backed by the firm's leadership. Champions are individuals who already innately share knowledge through their robust informal networks. Through this role, and using their existing connections, Learning and Knowledge Champions:

Raise awareness by promoting use of the Knowledge Gateway to find or submit key information and expertise.

Guide content development by mentoring team members on how to recognize and publish relevant content to the Knowledge Gateway. They help peers understand the submission process and follow the redaction guidelines to improve quality of submitted content.

Leverage knowledge resources such as subject matter specialists, news, and research services found within the Knowledge Management portal.

They do not function as help desk staff or submissions secretaries. Instead, Learning and Knowledge Champions harness the power of their networks to educate coworkers and help develop a widening culture of knowledge sharing. Buy-in to WFP's behaviors spreads quickly and organically. The growing WFP practice benefits from these well-developed hives of collaboration focused around their client service teams. Starting in December of 2007, 13 knowledge-savvy practitioners began leveraging their professional networks to bring knowledge owners and knowledge seekers together in WFP. They quickly found others who wanted to participate, and a group of deputy knowledge champions organically formed to support the program. Today, a volunteer network of over 40 professionals is aligned to client account teams and represents a coordinated effort to support KM across the practice.

Learning and Knowledge Champions teach the onboarding sessions for new hires, seizing an opportunity to integrate KM awareness and training into the start of PwC careers. The WFP KM program keeps encouraging connections and knowledge sharing across the practice to continue to support a more distinctive PwC experience for our clients.

LEADING PRACTICE: WEB 2.0 THE FUTURE OF KM?(!)

In the summer 2008 issue of PwC's *Technology Forecast*, an entire chapter is focused on Operational Web 2.0 in recognition that it is potentially the future of knowledge management. Web 2.0 is the term widely used to describe the social software enabling people to interact and share information through various media such as blogs, wikis, social networking, and mashups. Web 2.0 can empower knowledge workers and support programs that address knowledge retention through its unique ability to devolve authority, democratize information, and remove silos. As WFP initiatives encompass more levels of knowledge management maturity, employees are encouraged to explore the possibility of integrating Web 2.0 into the capture, transfer, retention, and creation of knowledge. For instance, Web 2.0 could support knowledge retention activities through all levels, from expert to novice. WFP can leverage various formal and informal networks for strategic decision making, innovation, and problem solving. Web 2.0 could also increase data analysis efficiency, transparency, and reuse of assets, as well as eliminate duplication of effort through the sharing of lessons learned. The opportunity is to recognize and mitigate the looming challenges of the departing Baby Boomer generation and adapt to the mobile aspects of the new generation of workers entering the workforce. Capitalizing on these changes will have an advantage over those who discover their problems only through the pain of diminished production—or worse—mission failure.

REFERENCES

Liebowitz, J. (2009). *Knowledge Retention: Strategies and Solutions*, Boca Raton, FL: Taylor & Francis/CRC Press.

Moore, J. (2009). Knowledge retention helps agencies retain employees' expertise, *Federal Computer Work*, www.fcw.com, April 17.

9

Gaining Competitive Advantage through Relationships

Whether voiced by well-known author Thomas Friedman or others, an essential key for companies is to develop and maintain public–private relationships. This is echoed by the Booz Allen Hamilton CEO Summit whereby summit attendees concluded that public–private relationships should be redefined to align with the new operating reality (Gerencser et al., 2008). Gerencser et al. (2008) use the term "megacommunities" to indicate the need for leaders and members of communities of organizations to cross boundaries to achieve goals they cannot achieve alone. In this sense, developing and maintaining relationships is a critical tenet for megacommunities to succeed. Megacommunities are dynamic versus the static nature of most public–private partnerships (PPPs) (Gerencser et al., 2008). The new style of leadership, as Walter Isaacson, CEO of The Aspen Institute states, "is as effective at facilitating cooperation among leaders in other sectors and organizations as it is within one's own organization" (Gerencser et al., 2008).

Relationship building must be used internally within management and employees in the organization, and externally with one's customers, stakeholders, third-party vendors, and the like. Kim Gordon talks about seven key strategies for building stronger relationships with customers (http://www.entrepreneur.com/marketing/marketingcolumnistkimtgordon/article66228.html):

1. Communicate frequently.
2. Offer customer rewards.
3. Hold special events.
4. Build two-way communication.
5. Enhance your customer service.

6. Launch multicultural programs.
7. Visit the trenches.

Actually, these strategies can also hold true for building stronger connections within the organization. Without performing these types of strategies, early warning signs of a failing company reputation can appear, as shown below (Burson-Marsteller, 2006):

Early Warning Signs of a Failing Reputation

Burson-Marsteller (2006)

1. There is low employee morale.
2. Internal politics are more important than doing the job well.
3. Top executives depart.
4. CEO celebrity displaces CEO credibility.
5. Employees speak of customers as nuisances.
6. Employees stop telling positive stories about the company.
7. Leaders stifle initiative.
8. Leaders talk about growth but focus on cost-cutting.
9. Bureaucratic procedures impede flexibility.
10. There is a tendency toward superficiality.
11. Problem-makers outnumber problem-solvers.
12. Internal documents leak.
13. There are few rewards and recognition.
14. Management spends more time inside than outside headquarters.
15. Employees spend too much time writing internal memos.

CONNECTIONS: THE INFORMAL ORGANIZATION

One of the earlier chapters focused on social networking and the importance of making connections. In a sense, relationship building is really "making connections." In the recent book, *Leading Outside the Lines: How to Mobilize the (In)Formal Organization, Energize Your Team, and Get Better Results* (Katzenbach and Khan, 2010), the informal organization is emphasized where most of the connections and relationships are built that allow for organizational success. Both the formal organizational chart and the informal organizational structure, working together, are needed to ensure a competitive advantage for the organization. Katzenbach and Khan (2010) stress the importance for CEOs to use the informal networks to tap into elements of the organization that they normally could not reach through the formal side (Clarke, 2010). Clarke (2010) talks about identifying the key influencers and central connectors in the organization. Companies such as Southwest Airlines, Apple, and Microsoft combine the informal networks with strategic and performance objectives and these organizations are successful partly because they have an informal organization that works so well (Katzenbach and Khan, 2010).

The informal organization does not have to be just employees internal to the organization. It can also extend beyond the boundaries of the employee base. For example, informal networks can exist between employees and outside supplier contacts, which may not be the designated official points of contact but could be those where a relationship has been built over time with the employee to get things done. Outsourcing arrangements can be part of the formal organizational procedures, but there may be certain individuals within the external outsourcing firm that one can count on more than others. This knowledge may invoke an informal network with those individuals.

Over the years, many organizations have turned to online communities of practice in order to increase collaboration and communication, and further develop a stronger sense of community and belonging. According to McDermott and Archibald (2010):

> We've observed this shift in our consulting work and in our research. This research was conducted with the Knowledge and Innovation Network at Warwick Business School and funded by the Warwick Innovative Manufacturing Research Centre and by Schlumberger, an oil-field services company. To examine the health and impact of communities, we did a quantitative study of 52 communities in 10 industries, and a qualitative assessment of more than 140 communities in a dozen organizations, consisting of interviews with support staff, leaders, community members, and senior management.

> The communities at construction and engineering giant Fluor illustrate the extent of the change. Global communities have replaced the company's distributed functional structure. Project teams remain the primary

organizational unit, however, 44 discipline- and industry-focused communities, with 24,000 active members, support the teams. The communities provide all functional services: creating guidelines for work practices and procedures; publishing technical documents; and offering career development, access to expert advice, and help with technical questions. They are the first and best source for technical knowledge at Fluor.

Some people may say that having informal networks and online communities helps organizations in moving toward being an "agile organization." Atkinson and Moffat (2005) talk about the movement from complexity to networks to effects to agility. Here, they argue that agility is related to network-centric organizations. In this sense, organizations push "power to the edge" whereby agility is defined by the attributes of responsiveness, robustness, innovativeness, flexibility, adaptability, and resiliency.

SYNERGY: THE WHOLE IS GREATER THAN THE SUM OF THE PARTS

As we have mentioned in previous chapters, an organization's strategic human capital includes not only the employees and management of the organization, but also the contractors, subcontractors, consultants, public–private partners, third-party suppliers, academic partners, outsourcing firms, and other relationships that are key to the organization's success. All these components are built upon relationships, and when integrated effectively, the synergistic effect produces a "stronger" organization as a whole.

Watching the National Basketball Association games, synergy plays an all-important role. A team may have many superstars, but if they cannot gel as a team on the court, then they will be suboptimizing. Similarly, if the organization is not clicking on all fronts, then it may be suboptimizing as well. Relationships with one's customers are essential in order to promote retention, referrals, and increased spending (http://www.dbmarketing.com/articles/Art110.htm). Many companies are using online social media in order to further reach out and strengthen the bond between the customer and the organization. Social media are being used heavily for relationship management. For example, according to a blog posting (http://blog.optimum7.com/melissa/social-media/using-social-media-for-relationship-marketing.html):

Best Buy has set up Twelp Force, a dedicated Twitter page that is used to answer tech-related questions to current and potential customers about their products.

Pepsi has developed a multi-channel campaign that includes a very attractive Twitter page, an official Facebook page, and a Refresh Blog where they run, for example, a campaign where they give away grants to people with "refreshing ideas."

Gartner predicts by 2016 companies will need to coordinate social customer relationship management, internal communication, and coordination with the public social networking site plans to enable integration into a comprehensive strategy (http://itworld.journalspace.com/2010/12/01/gartner-predicted-in-2011-the-top-ten-strategic-technology/).

In the near term, organizations will need to take advantage of relationship management techniques in order to remain competitive in the marketplace. Social media will continue to have a strong presence, especially in further developing relationships with customers. Developing and maintaining these relationships will bear fruit for organizations to harvest in the future.

The next section describes a case study at Northrop Grumman that focuses on the importance of developing and maintaining relationships for competitive advantage.

Case Study: Creating Competitive Advantage Through Building Relationships

Scott Shaffar and Bob Payne
Northrop Grumman Corporation

INTRODUCTION

Facebook, LinkedIn, and other social networking tools are without doubt changing the way people view their personal networks (those associated with activities other than work) and professional networks (those associated with one's line of work). Creating and maintaining a network or interconnected system of people is not sufficient for creating competitive advantage. Relationships on the other hand are key to competitive advantage, and involve our networks, but go beyond the simple connection with another person to include some sort of dependence, alliance, affinity, or kinship. Professional relationships are most often formed through shared work experiences such as working on the same project. They could also be formed by simply working at the same physical location, or having a customer–supplier dependence. Relationships usually require time to strengthen and are a strong function of mutual trust. Initial trust can be gained by being associated with the same company, or better yet, being on the same team, whereby mere membership yields an initial level of trust. We also know that trust takes time to build, but that it can be destroyed quickly.

In the next few pages, we share stories of how building networks and relationships provides a means by which competitive advantage is achieved, and profit gained.

We divide relationships into two primary categories: internal and external. By internal we mean relationships involving one's own organization. Examples could be members from the same department, business unit, or company. External typically means beyond one's own organization. Examples would include another company within the same industry or suppliers to your company.

BUILDING AND LEVERAGING INTERNAL RELATIONSHIPS

Starting a knowledge management (KM) initiative from scratch in a large and complex engineering company such as Northrop Grumman should seem like a daunting task. In a company where hard technical and programmatic data drive decision making, asking the folks that make these decisions to start thinking about knowledge and its importance to the distant future takes more than persistence, it takes relationships. Some relationships are developed through preparation and being able to see and then seize the opportunity. Other relationships take strategic planning and cultivation. Whether opportunistic or strategic, the road to building KM at Northrop Grumman was accelerated by these relationships.

In 1998, the B-2 bomber program had ended production, and the company was consequently reducing its staff by roughly 90%. Scott Shaffar, then an engineer on that program, realized that there was a risk of knowledge loss, especially given the fact that the company knew there would be a long-term upgrade and maintenance business for these aircraft. Shaffar approached Dan Cockroft, the B-2 program human resources director with the idea of a project to address this knowledge loss. Cockroft supported the idea and recommended that Shaffar team with Bob Payne, who at the time was working a critical skills identification project for the B-2 program. Within weeks,

Cockroft sponsored Shaffar and Payne to present a knowledge management proposal to Scott Seymour, then program manager for the B-2 program. The result of that presentation was agreement to move forward aggressively. This turned out to be the start of a decade-long journey and a strong network and relationship among Shaffar, Payne, Cockroft, and Seymour, that created competitive advantage in a number of areas for Northrop Grumman.

Shaffar and Payne went on to form many additional internal relationships on the B-2 program as the KM effort required support from the entire B-2 program management team. One of these key relationships was with Jeff Wessels, an engineering manager who took on the task of working with Shaffar and Payne to mitigate the risk of knowledge loss across B-2 engineering. This also turned out to be a pivotal moment in internal relationship building in that Wessels later led the KM effort for the former Air Combat Systems division and subsequently held a number of key engineering management roles.

As part of building their KM expertise, Shaffar and Payne attended a number of external KM conferences, which in the late 1990s were plentiful. Connections and relationships made at these conferences were critical to their fledgling KM effort. Two initial relationships from these meetings that provided immediate payoff were with Adrian Ward, KM manager from Hughes Space and Communications and Bill Spencer a KM manager from the National Security Agency. Ward and Spencer were key subject matter experts applying KM at their respective organizations. Each KM leader was targeting different business results both of which were seen as resonating with the B-2 Program for Northrop Grumman.

In the late 1980s, competition in the communications satellite market was fierce as the race to launch constellations of mobile communications satellites was on.* Hughes Space and Communications, now part of Boeing, was at the center of an intense competition to build and launch these satellites. Ward's story was about how KM was being used to help Hughes decrease the time to market for new satellites to meet the growing demand for satellites on orbit. Spencer had a different story, one of bringing a new more collaborative and knowledge-sharing management approach to a traditional, high-security environment where important institutional and deep cultural barriers

---

* Abrahms, D. (1997). Seven iridium satellites ride Russian rocket into orbit. *The Washington Times.* Washington DC. (June 19)

to sharing information were being addressed. After meeting Shaffar and Payne, both Ward and Spencer agreed to share their stories with the B-2 program executive leadership team. Once again, Shaffar and Payne found themselves in front of Seymour's team, this time with Ward and Spencer as guest speakers. The insight from these presentations built an understanding of the business value of KM to addressing the critical need to mitigate the looming knowledge loss as the program transitioned from producing new B-2 aircraft to supporting and upgrading the fleet in the field. That meeting also provided Shaffar and Payne credibility in the eyes of Seymour and his teams because Ward and Spencer had confirmed their plans were on the right path.

Shaffar and Payne also met other Northrop Grumman employees at these conferences. Most important, they became aware of a group within Northrop Grumman's information technology (IT) sector that was providing KM solutions to the U.S. government. The business development director for that effort was John Seaberg who, along with Shaffar and Payne, began getting calls from other people from across Northrop Grumman who were working with or interested in KM. They decided to create a Northrop Grumman KM community of practice. At the first meeting in 2000, roughly 20 attendees arrived, some of whom traveled across the country for the meeting (on their own budget). This small group later grew to well over 600 members and attracted attention in 2004 as the result of hosting the largest internal conference in the company's history at the time (with over 300 attendees).

In late 2001, Shaffar and Seymour met with Kent Kresa, then Northrop Grumman's CEO, in Kresa's office to discuss their KM work. Kresa in turn directed that a briefing be provided to his leadership team, the Northrop Grumman Corporate Policy Council (CPC). This drew the interest of the IT sector president, and because Shaffar was already working with Seaberg, it was decided that he and John would jointly provide that briefing. Their recommendations to the CPC called for the creation of a corporate KM Council that would provide leadership for this new program. The CPC agreed to Shaffar and Seaberg's recommendations and all of the sector presidents appointed representatives. By 2001, the Northrop Grumman KM Council was fully established and well underway in developing KM solutions for the company. In roughly a four-year span (1998 to 2001), Shaffar had gone from an idea for the B-2 bomber program to a corporatewide, CEO-sponsored effort. That rapid growth happened because Shaffar formed relationships with key leaders, including, Cockroft, Wessels, Seaberg, Seymour, Payne, and many others.

The Corporate KM Council went on to develop a number of KM solutions for the company, including a single collaboration and document management system called ShareCenter, which today serves the company with over 50,000 active users. The Corporate KM Council also provided a new search engine, and introduced the concept of communities of practice across the company. Today there are hundreds of active Northrop Grumman communities. Certainly this work required a tremendous expansion of the networks and relationships of Shaffar, Payne, Wessels, and Seaberg. This included many people from across Northrop Grumman, as well as KM industry suppliers and KM professionals from other companies and organizations.

Shaffar, Payne, Wessels, and Seaberg did not realize that their ideas and work in the late 1990s would grow so rapidly into the creation of a formal Corporate KM Council, a 300+ active member companywide KM community of practice, a dedicated, full-time KM team, and a journey that would last over a decade. Key to this growth and sustainment was executive sponsorship, which was provided throughout that decade by Seymour and Cockroft. Seymour was promoted to the position of Air Combat Systems business-area general manager, and then later to the president of the Integrated Systems sector. Through each successive position, Seymour continued sponsoring the KM initiative. Cockroft was likewise promoted and continued as a key supporter of KM, providing the important human resources partnership. To this day, Shaffar, Payne, Wessels, and Seaberg work at Northrop Grumman, albeit in different jobs, and fortunately their careers have progressed nicely. Most important, they now have over a decade of friendship and shared experiences. There are numerous other companywide relationships formed in the early years of their KM work that the four of them enjoy today.

LEVERAGING INTERNAL RELATIONSHIPS FOR BUSINESS ADVANTAGE

To further illustrate the competitive advantage of internal relationships, we share two stories about Northrop Grumman products that benefited from the relationships created for the B-2 bomber and corporatewide KM initiatives: the Jupiter Icy Moons Orbiter (JIMO) spacecraft, and the BQM-74 Navy target.

THE JUPITER ICY MOONS ORBITER STORY

In March 2004, Peggy Nelson, JIMO program manager, reached out to Seymour to request support for an upcoming proposal to NASA JPL for a nuclear-powered spacecraft to the Icy Moons of Jupiter. The JIMO project, later known as Prometheus, was planned to be launched in 2013, would take 20 years to transit to Jupiter, and conduct data gathering on arrival at the moon Ganymede. Northrop was competing with Lockheed, the incumbent, and Boeing for the contract. The request for proposal (RFP) included a request for KM to architect the data, information, and knowledge so that when the spacecraft arrived and began to conduct its science mission, the operators would have access to the spacecraft builder's data, information, and knowledge generated while constructing the instruments 20 years earlier. Seymour passed the request for support to Shaffar. On reading the RFP, it became clear that the writer of the RFP had used the JPL KM program as a reference point. Additional research into the JPL KM approach quickly became helpful in recognizing the language and themes of how an effective KM strategy could be fashioned and integrated into the Northrop Grumman JIMO proposal. The internal relationship to Seymour enabled an appreciation of importance of KM to the offering and leverage to assign Payne to develop the KM section of the proposal and become the knowledge architect on the program. The KM section of the proposal became an integration of many of the best KM practices and tools that had evolved within the corporation over the previous 6 years.

On September 20, 2004, in a stunning come-from-behind victory, Northrop Grumman was awarded the Prometheus contract. The section on knowledge management was cited by the source selection board as one of several strengths that helped Northrop Grumman win the competition. As it turned out, several JPL program leaders were involved in the early stages of KM at JPL. Unfortunately, due to a change in administrators and priorities at NASA the following June 2005 the project was canceled.

THE BQM-74 TARGETS STORY

In 2006, Mike McCormack, manager of targets production, was faced with the first of several technicians, with more than 30 years experience, retiring from the BQM-74 production line. The BQM-74, a target program for the U.S. Navy, had been in continuous production since the early 1980s building thousands of targets. These retiring workers would soon be leaving, taking much of their critical tacit or undocumented knowhow of building these targets with them. Along with John Salafia, the targets program director, and Steve Mastin, program manager, they became concerned with the risk of losing a generation of production workers nearing retirement. Earlier in 1997, both McCormack and Salafia had become acquainted with the ability of KM to capture and transfer knowledge to mitigate the risk of knowledge loss as experienced workers left the B-2 program during the transition from production to support. Salafia went on to become the program director of the targets program, the Northrop Grumman-built BQM-74 target for the U.S. Navy. McCormack contacted Shaffar who assigned two KM team project managers, Gina DiAmbrosia and Mark Britton, to develop a process for videotaping the technicians explaining the important tips and tricks needed to build the target efficiently and free of defects. Many hundreds of hours of recorded video later, a set of 40 hours of the most important processes were published. The program and production team at the manufacturing center in Palmdale, California set an expectation and requirement for all new hires to sit through all 40 hours of the video before they were authorized to begin work on the targets production line. As a result, the small staff of retiring technicians was succeeded by a crop of young technicians who picked up where their predecessors left off without an increase of defects or drop in efficiency.

BUILDING EXTERNAL RELATIONSHIPS, INCLUDING WITH YOUR COMPETITORS

In addition to realizing the value from internal relationships, we have also found great value in developing external relationships with other knowledge management practitioners, especially those within the aerospace and defense industry. An example of this is when Shaffar and Payne formed a relationship with Ward and Spencer which in turn provided confidence for Seymour and his team in supporting the use of knowledge management for their B-2 program. Clearly an advantage to forming such relationships is that companies within the same industry often face identical challenges. A common challenge across the aerospace and defense industry is a bimodal age distribution with the largest percentage of the workforce at or near retirement eligibility (from late 40s to early 60s), and a secondary peak of employees, but relatively small in total, for employees under the age of 30.

Moreover, the aerospace and defense industry commonly suffers from a gap in this distribution at mid-career point (ages 30 to 40) due to the industry funding cuts in the late 1990s. Naturally this bimodal age distribution presents challenges in knowledge loss due to retirements as well as knowledge transfer across a large age, experience, and generational gap (retirement to entry level). In addition to common knowledge management challenges, our industry has similar organizational constructs and general operating principles that are largely driven by defense acquisition regulation. This includes strict rules on funding mechanisms, relatively low discretionary funding pools, security concerns, programmatic firewalls, and bust and boom business cycles. These operating principles present challenges to the implementation of knowledge management solutions.

During the last decade we have found and formed relationships with other KM leaders in our industry. In addition to Ward and Spencer, we created relationships concentrated in California with Kiho Sohn, Pratt & Whitney (formerly Boeing) Rocketdyne in Canoga Park, Stew Sutton, The Aerospace Corporation in Manhattan Beach, and Jeanne Holm, NASA JPL in Pasadena. These relationships were largely formed through getting to know each other from KM-related groups and conferences. In 2005, given our connections as well as geographical proximity, we decided to start a Southern California aerospace and defense knowledge management community of practice made up of members from our four teams (Northrop Grumman, Boeing, The Aerospace Corporation, and NASA). We established an informal and low-impact (cost and planning) approach to our meetings, which included rotations among the participants' locations, and lasting a half day, from 10 a.m. to 2 p.m. to allow for commute time across Los Angeles. Our meetings had a standard schedule of networking, presentations, lunch plus networking, and sometimes splitting up into small groups on specific KM topics of interest.

Initial reaction within our companies to forming this community was caution and even in one case, strong resistance because the members of this proposed community were viewed as competitors. Indeed, the aerospace and defense industry is one where we are often competing fiercely on one contract and teammates on yet another. Nevertheless, there is a constant concern of competitive advantage. The viewpoint shared among the founders of this community of practice was that any competitive advantage to be gained from KM would be driven by our prospective organization's ability to implement knowledge management solutions, not from the knowledge of these solutions. We also had the common vision that the intelligent application of knowledge management within the defense and aerospace industry is ultimately the right thing to do for our nation. We knew that we all faced very difficult challenges, and that by combining our knowledge, skills, and experience, we would ultimately bring greater success to our respective organizations. Losing a contract due to knowledge shared from this group seemed very unlikely.

Indeed, we were able to get past this initial resistance and move forward with our community. We have since formed very close friendships, shared many enjoyable meals and events, and have learned much from each other. Our group meetings also served as an important counseling session for each of us as we were able to talk about our challenges and realize we were not alone in our journeys. This group also aided in career development and spurred local academic offerings including a graduate program in knowledge management at California State University-Northridge, KM research at the University of California-Irvine, the University of Southern California, as well as a yearly KM conference hosted by Pepperdine University.

FIVE COMMON THEMES

The stories we have shared on creating competitive advantage through building relationships have the following five common themes:

1. *Relationships take time.* Building relationships requires time because a key is the development of mutual trust.
2. *It takes a diverse and strong network.* Success in business requires a diverse network that connects oneself with many others who have a variety of skills, knowledge, and experience. It also requires a strong network with positive relationships.
3. *Let your network shine in your light.* Relationships need to be mutually beneficial. When one drives for success and leverages one's network and relationships, it is critical that once success is achieved, it is shared, even if it means that the success becomes largely attributable to others. Letting them shine in your light will ultimately pay off, especially when you call on your network to join you in the future on a new endeavor.

4. *It is a long-term investment.* Another theme to the stories we have shared is that they took place over a long period of time, especially when the formation of the network and relationships is considered. The KM journey at Northrop Grumman took more than a decade and the network and relationships developed early on were critical throughout that journey.

5. *Internal and external networks and relationships are both required.* Our experience has demonstrated great benefit from both internal and external networks and relationships. For large complex organizations, internal networks are normally the priority. We have also found great value in external relationships, especially those within our industry.

BACKGROUND

Northrop Grumman

Northrop Grumman Corporation is a leading global security company whose 75,000 employees provide innovative systems, products, and solutions in aerospace, electronics, information systems, and technical services to government and commercial customers worldwide.* Please visit www.northropgrumman.com for more information.

B-2 Spirit Bomber

The U.S. Air Force's B-2, also known as the Stealth Bomber, is the flagship of the nation's long-range strike arsenal, and one of the most survivable aircraft in the world. Its unique capabilities, including its stealth characteristics, allow it to penetrate the most sophisticated defenses and hold at risk high-value, heavily defended enemy targets. The B-2 has demonstrated its capabilities in several combat scenarios, most recently during Operation Iraqi Freedom.

Northrop Grumman, the B-2 prime contractor, leads an industry team that is working with the Air Force to modernize the B-2 to ensure that it remains fully mission capable against evolving worldwide threats. A range of upgrade programs are improving the B-2's lethality; its ability to collect, process, and disseminate battlefield information with joint force commanders or other local first respond-

---

* (2011). "Northrop Grumman: A Leader in Global Security." Retrieved 3/11/2011, from http://www.northropgrumman.com/.

ers worldwide; and its ability to receive updated target information during a mission.[*]

BQM-74E Aerial Target

The BQM-74E is a turbojet-powered aerial target with high-performance capabilities. Although emulation of enemy antiship cruise missiles is the primary mission, others include simulation of aircraft for training naval aviators in air-to-air combat and support of the test and evaluation of new weapon systems. The BQM-74E and its ground support system are highly portable. This attribute enables shipboard operations in support of deployed naval combatants where maximum flexibility and rapid turnaround are required.[†]

REFERENCES

Atkinson, S. and Moffat, J. (2005). The Agile Organization: From Informal Networks to Complex Effects and Agility, Command and Control Research Program, Washington, D.C., *www.dodccrp.org/files/Atkinson_Agile.pdf.*

Burson-Marsteller (2006). Cures for the Company Blues: A Pocket Guide for Leaders, *www.ceogo.com/documents/Cures_book_final.pdf.*

Clarke, K. (2010). The Secret Life of Your Association, Associations Now, American Society of Association Executives, Washington, DC, December.

Gerencser, M., van Lee, R., Napolitano, F., and Kelly, C. (2008). *Megacommunities: How Leaders of Government, Business, and Non-Profits Can Tackle Today's Global Challenges Together,* New York: Palgrave Macmillan.

Katzenbach, J. and Khan, Z. (2010). *Leading Outside the Lines: How to Mobilize the (in) Formal Organization, Energize Your Team, and Get Better Results,* New York: Jossey-Bass.

McDermott, R. and Archibald, D. (2010). Harnessing your staff's informal networks, *Harvard Business Review,* March, http://hbr.org/2010/03/harnessing-your-staffs-informal-networks/ar/1.

---

[*] (2011). "B-2 Spirit Bomber." Retrieved 3/10/2011, from http://www.as.northropgrumman.com/products/b2spirit/index.html.

[†] (2011). "BQM-74E Aerial Target." Retrieved 3/11/2011, from http://www.as.northropgrumman.com/products/targets_bqm74e/index.html.

10

Gaining Competitive Advantage through Innovation

In today's competitive white waters, organizations must continue to innovate to survive. As a nation, the United States has some challenges in terms of an eroding scientific edge. According to Bryan Walsh of *Time* magazine (2010), the United States has challenges to overcome from a scientific and innovative standpoint:

> A landmark report released in May by the National Science Board lays out the numbers: while U.S. investment in R&D as a share of total GDP has remained relatively constant since the mid-1980s at 2.7%, the federal share of R&D has been consistently declining—even as Asian nations like Japan and South Korea have rapidly increased that ratio. China's investments in R&D grew more than 20% a year between 1996 and 2007, compared with less than 6% annual growth in the U.S. At the same time, American students seem to be losing interest in science—only about one-third of U.S. bachelor's degrees are in science or engineering now, compared with 63% in Japan and 53% in China. ... Once the undisputed leader, the U.S. is now lagging as a hot spot for innovation." (Walsh, 2010; p. 42)

OPEN INNOVATION

According to Chesbrough (2003), who fostered the idea, "open innovation" is combining internal and external ideas as well as internal and external paths to market to advance the development of new technologies. The thrust of this approach, as opposed to traditional closed innovation, is that companies need to work with smart people inside and outside the company and the business model must support these types of external relationships. In Chapter 9, we talked about the importance of developing and maintaining relationships. Unilever, for example, has been a strong advocate of open innovation, or what they call, collaborative innovation. They indicate that "smart collaboration between ourselves and our partners allows us to leverage a greater mix of technologies and speed up time to market to deliver value none of us could achieve on our own" (http://www.unilever.com/innovation/collaborating/). Procter & Gamble's Connect+Develop Program uses open innovation and has established more than 1,000 active agreements with innovation partners (https://secure3.verticali.net/pg-connection-portal/ctx/noauth/PortalHome.do). Of course, the open innovation efforts should be tailored to the company and its culture. And now, with Web 2.0 tools, open innovation is augmented through having online communities, social networking, and other collaborative social media techniques at one's disposal for generating new ideas.

INNOVATION SUCCESS FACTORS

Tim Brown (2011), the CEO of the innovation consultancy IDEO, states that:

> When people talk about building a culture of innovation, they tend to focus on what's happening inside a company—and that's clearly part of it. At IDEO we're looking at how to build our clients' capacity for continual innovation through organizational design. But permission to innovate also involves the culture an organization creates out in the world. (http://hbr.org/web/extras/hbr-agenda-2011/tim-brown)

In August 2010 IDEO launched a site called OpenIDEO, an open innovation network/online community where people can create solutions to some of the world's toughest challenges (http://openideo.com/). OpenIDEO's mantra is, "Where people design better, together."

In order to promote innovation in organizations, the chief innovation officer or the vice president of innovation title has been created in recent years. According to research by Accenture (Koetzier and Alon, 2009), having a chief innovation officer can make a difference. Certainly, ideas are less likely to be put aside when there is an internal champion in charge of innovation. According to Alon (2010), there are 10 key ways that businesses can improve innovation:

1. Conceive of innovation as a business discipline, and then manage and execute it systematically.
2. Craft a precise definition of innovation's role in the overall corporate strategy based on the company's industry, market, and competitive environment. And specify the types of innovation being sought to build a sustainable competitive position, and the specific value the innovations are expected to generate.
3. Focus much more time and resources on breakthrough, long-term, game-changing innovation.
4. Take more risks, reward failure, and encourage continuous improvement.
5. Measure innovation performance and results as you do other business functions such as marketing, strategy, and operations.
6. Focus on the customer experience and less on technology.
7. Embrace open innovation and open innovation tools.
8. Encourage idea generation from everywhere, both inside and outside your company.
9. Consider appointing a chief innovation officer and setting up a uniformity of command for corporate innovation accountability.
10. Have a dedicated budget for innovation.

Booz & Company conducted their annual Global Innovation 1000 Study. In their 2010 Global Innovation Study, pharmaceutical giant Roche Holding took the top position for innovation spending. In fact, healthcare companies took 5 of the top 10 spots on the list and 7 of the top 20. Microsoft (number 2), Nokia (number 3), and Pfizer (number 5) rounded out the top five (Wall, 2010). According to Wall (2010) and Booz & Company, "The survey found that companies that focus on a set of innovation capabilities most consistent with their innovation strategy and tightly aligned with their overall corporate strategy outperform their rivals. Companies in the Global Innovation 1000 that take such a coherent approach to capabilities reported higher profit margins than their competitors, by up to 22%." Innovation executives were separately surveyed about which companies they considered to be the most innovative. Their top three responses were Apple, Google, and then 3M (Jaruzelski and Dehoff, 2010).

Fostering an innovative culture combines many of the aspects that we have previously discussed in earlier chapters. Certainly, knowledge management plays a role in terms of leveraging knowledge internally and externally to spawn new ideas. One of the major reasons organizations engage in knowledge management is to increase innovation. Social networking and collaboration are also instrumental in generating creative ideas. In open innovation, reaching out to external customers and partners is beneficial to the organization for developing new products or services. Relationship building, discussed in the previous chapter, leads to innovation and most of the elements we have highlighted in other chapters—technology, human capital, analytics, and others—all are part of the innovation process.

With this said, why are so many organizations less innovative than others? Part of the equation is hiring smart people. Steve Jobs of Apple states (http://money.cnn.com/galleries/2008/fortune/0803/gallery.jobsqna.fortune/3.html):

> It's not about pop culture, and it's not about fooling people, and it's not about convincing people that they want something they don't. We figure out what we want. And I think we're pretty good at having the right discipline to think through whether a lot of other people are going to want it, too. That's what we get paid to do. So you can't go out and ask people, you know, what's the next big (thing.) There's a great quote by Henry Ford, right? He said, "If I'd have asked my customers what they wanted, they would have told me 'A faster horse.'"

Another part of the equation is to have a culture that promotes innovative ideas. Many of these ideas require risks. Leadership has to encourage risk-taking and not penalize people for failing. Many CEOs hire senior leaders not simply for what successes they have achieved but also for what valuable lessons they have learned from previous failures. Mark Zuckerberg, the CEO of Facebook, was asked about the secret to his company's success. He replied, "Boldness, speed, and focus" (http://www.businessinsider.com/henry-blodget-the-secret-to-facebooks-success-2009-8). Without having the right people and the right culture, companies will have difficulties innovating. Many CEOs and senior leaders are focused more on the market, the short-term versus the long-term. As such, fewer resources may be put into research and development and that may lessen the likelihood for innovation to emerge.

LOOKING TOWARD THE FUTURE

As the world continues to become "flatter," companies will need to innovate faster in order to outpace the global competition. Having an innovation process, change agents, increased R&D resources, and a chief innovation officer will further help organizations in developing new ideas for products or services. Even fairly conservative organizations have chief innovation officers, such as Sheldon Laube at the international accounting and consulting firm PricewaterhouseCoopers (PwC). About two years ago, PwC launched iPlace in order to share ideas and innovate via an online idea management platform. In the first year, there were over 2,000 ideas, 10,000 comments, and 40,000 votes (http://pwcinnovate.wordpress.com/2010/07/23/pwc-iplace-six-factors-to-our-success/). PwC has an innovation blog as well in order to share opinions and discuss the latest innovation happenings in the firm. Other organizations have, and will, follow suit to find ways to generate discussion, collaboration, and sharing of ideas for knowledge generation. Even conferences are using crowdsourcing (using social media to vote using the "wisdom of the crowd" phenomenon) in order to get the conference's intended audiences to vote on which topics and abstracts would most interest them for conference presentations. The years ahead look fruitful for those organizations that continue to innovate, even during recessionary periods, so that they will be farther ahead of their competition once out of the recessions.

In the next section, Greg Downing, John Kools, and Joanne Andreadis discuss how innovation is being achieved in the government, especially as related to health and human services.

Fostering Innovation to Create Public Value: A Government Perspective

Gregory J. Downing,* John J. Kools,† and Joanne D. Andreadis†
*U.S. Department of Health and Human Services (HHS)
†Centers for Disease Control and Prevention (CDC)

BACKGROUND

The newcomer to government service might be quite surprised to find herself captured within a cauldron of innovation. Government agencies are often in a constant struggle to improve and this is fueled, in part, by factors uncommon to private sector experiences in business, academia, and nongovernmental organizations. The political processes themselves represent a perpetual generator of change reflecting public opinion, and equipped with a known timecycle of renewal based on the voice of the electorate. Each new leadership team has new ideas and priorities that will drive better service, more efficient and effective operations, and greater value for public investment. The legacies of government are often captured as the "great transformations" such as the New Deal, Civil Rights, Title IX, and Americans with Disabilities Act that at their origins reflect change in the course of society toward new goals, ambitions, and successes against inequities. The nature of government then, in and of itself, serves as an implementation arm for the public's ambitions to motivate change. This case characterizes the elements of renewal, how the government leader charts a course for innovation in the roles that he or she serves, from policymaker to program manager, budget analyst, or political appointee.

At first glimpse, the question of competitive advantage raises a question, "Compete with whom?" The American culture is highly competitive: where in government do we see competition? In some cases, American innovation is sparked by a particular cause or mission, such as to improve safety, to seek new knowledge, or to achieve technological advances that improve the quality of life. The political processes are often motivated by competition for the "best ideas" and opportunities to become more efficient or prosperous as a nation. Throughout history, great feats have been undertaken toward sharpening this competitive edge.

The Department of Health and Human Services' (HHS) environment serves as a good case study for understanding the forces of innovation at work. From the standpoint of competition, the challenge is to outperform the past with an eye on competing with the future. In large part, the economic forces for healthcare costs in the United States present unprecedented financial obligations, with projections of healthcare costs representing over 20% of our nation's gross national product in the next few years.[1] Obligations for future healthcare cost increases related in part to the financial burdens of new technology and aging demographics are commonly portrayed as a threat to U.S. economic stability, and potentially national security. At the same time, the current medical care system provides little incentive for innovation. The payment systems based on volume rather than quality and value and inadequate information about quality are the basis for market failure.[2]

The stakes are high for legislative and executive branches of government and the private sector, and the stage has been set for new concepts of healthcare management, thereby opening many doors of opportunity for innovation.

The first thoughts about innovation in government might bring to mind the space age and roles that government and industry created in the 1960s toward a defense mission that yielded many societal benefits. Early federal agency innovation programs focused on the Department of Defense needs for connectivity and information sharing led to the innovations behind the Internet. Government often uses incentives (or penalties) as a means to catalyze innovation; modern day threats to our environment have led to incentives for the development of alternative energy sources, and improvements in efficiency (using methods such as tax incentives for renewable energy sources). In addition to incentives, government pays for new ideas, using grants, contracts, and occasionally prizes and challenges to drive change. In government, the innovation cycle is not all that dissimilar to that of other segments of our society and economy. Challenges are recognized, ideas are solicited and tested, and competitive forces drive the ingenuity for problem solving. Incentives are often assembled to drive adoption of winning ideas. Often, important ideas for improvements are produced and proven as bona fide solutions yet never adopted.[3] Cultural barriers, lack of education and understanding, and resistance to change from those who gain from existing methods need to be overcome. It turns out in many cases that the marketing and communication of an innovative idea or the acceptance of knowledge is of greater significance than the innovation itself. Another important factor that has tended to play an important role for government involvement in promoting innovation pertains to situations when there is market failure based on situations where the commercial gains do not sustain returns on investment needed, yet the public benefits achieved through the discoveries are of sufficient societal benefit to warrant the effort.

HHS is constituted of an array of 11 agencies with vastly different missions aimed at improving the health of the nation, and providing services that support those in society who are most in need. The missions span healthcare and service delivery, basic and applied R&D, public health services, regulatory oversight of products and processes, and account for over a quarter of the U.S. economy. The organization's workforce of nearly 70,000 employees is geographically distributed across the country in 10 regions in the United States and also internationally. There is a substantial emphasis on customer service with a high premium placed on communication and information services. In many ways, as a collective, its processes and governance structure make it a definitive source for data, information, and knowledge management. An important feature of successful government programs is the public trust that the knowledge and information provided is of high integrity. Managing information, facilitating its dissemination, and promoting the adoption of the information are key aspects of the knowledge management infrastructure.

In this case study, we examine the critical elements of innovation in government. The importance of leadership is addressed in identifying key characteristics of an organization's management that enable innovation through risk-taking, rewards, and hypothesis testing, and workforce engagement in the process. Underpinning the workforce innovation efforts are tools, projects, networks, and processes that can provide incentives, educational information, and experience in best practices. Collectively, these features represent ingredients that define a culture of innovation in government. The following in-depth view of one federal department's recent experience brings context to these values.

INNOVATION: ITS ORIGINS AND SOCIAL MOTIVATIONS

As Gordon Forward, former president and CEO of Chaparral Steel adroitly said, "To stand still is to fall behind." Innovation is a critical tool in gaining competitive advantage and an organization's innovation capacity is defined by its ability to connect ideas from a wide range of disciplines and the quality of its organizational networks and partners.[4] Thomas Edison is considered one of America's greatest innovators and the founding father of the modern R&D laboratory. His success was largely due to his ability to systematically collect and recombine knowledge to create new knowledge, understand unmet needs, and promote mainstream adoption of his inventions. His Menlo Park laboratory team focused on solving problems across many industries, growing their own capabilities by actively sharing information to learn from failure and build upon successes, and thinking about adoption early in development. Successful innovation within public organizations requires many of these same skills.

Innovation is also fundamentally about change and nurturing change management within organizations. Heath and Heath (2010) use a visual metaphor of an elephant, rider, and path to describe how to support change in ourselves and organizations.[5,6] The rider holding the reins is our rational analytic side requiring clear direction; the elephant which represents our culture and captures our emotional response to change can be motivated by confidence built upon tangible small successes and a larger sense of purpose that engages the entire organizational community; and the path traveled can be either supportive of change or laden with fallen trees, rocks, and other barriers.[6] In the next few paragraphs we explore tactics for informing the rider (leadership), motivating the elephant (fostering a culture of growth and learning), and shaping the path (processes and tools that facilitate innovation).

LEADERSHIP

VISION

Organizational leaders in government must identify innovation as a priority and clearly articulate the path forward in the form of goals to drive innovation that rapidly advances the mission. In 1961, President John F. Kennedy launched the United States toward the goal of "landing a man on the moon and returning him safely to the earth" before the end of the decade. Through this statement, the president articulated a clear and ambitious goal, a purpose that merited extraordinary contribution, and accountability through transparency. His leadership unleashed a national effort led by NASA that required deconstructing complex problems into achievable components, exchange of knowledge, and cross-organizational coordination on a scale never seen before that ultimately led to one of the most innovative periods in U.S. history. The 1961 speech is a great example of how a leader can create a clear and compelling vision that empowers and unifies people by tapping into their self-identity and providing enough information to make the goal attainable.

OPEN INNOVATION

Leaders interested in encouraging open innovation may also take steps to make organizational boundaries more porous.[7] On January 21, 2009, President Barack Obama issued a memorandum on the establishment of "a system of transparency, public participation, and collaboration" known as Open Government.[8] The aim of this initiative is to identify a course of action with the potential to reinvent government through innovation. Transparency provides information to citizens about what their government is doing and encourages accountability, participation by the public in the workings of government promotes better decision making, and collaboration encourages information exchange and partnership with the public and across sectors. Within just two years, Open Government has created a cascade of activity and experimentation within government that has vastly expanded the networks of individuals, communities, and organizations engaged in the health and welfare of the United States.

Some specific examples of HHS Open Government initiatives include transforming static strategic planning documents into dynamic management tools through public engagement and using these tools to emphasize innovation as an organizational priority (HHS Open Government Plan; HHS Strategic Plan 2010-2015);[9] creating transparent enterprise performance systems that allow the public and other stakeholders to monitor progress on key measures and allow policy makers and others to make informed decisions (FDA-TRACK, and Center for Medicare & Medicaid Services (CMS) Dashboard); creating new organizational structures with an eye on the future to enable new health delivery models to be created, tested, and evaluated for scalability (CMS Innovation Center); and exploiting investments in organizational assets such as health data, transactional information, and science through public access to promote their use, reuse, and application to unforeseen new products by individuals, entrepreneurs, or organizations from around the world.

TARGETED INNOVATION

Many public organizations have broad responsibilities and fostering decentralized organic innovation is important but may not be sufficient to support accelerated near-term progress in priority areas. In a bold move, the Centers for Disease Control and Prevention (CDC), an agency of HHS charged with preserving and protecting the health and safety of the nation, elevated 10 very specific outcome-oriented goals called Winnable Battles.[10] These winnable battles are public health priorities where CDC and the public health community can make significant progress within one to four years through a focused effort. This approach and the development of plans of action for each area not only create awareness about these topics but also focus government and nongovernment partners on collaborating and coordinating more effectively as they take action in these high priority areas. The domestic winnable battles include: healthcare-associated infections,

Human Immunodeficiency Virus (HIV) transmission, motor vehicle injuries, obesity/nutrition/food safety, teen and unintended pregnancy, and tobacco. These specific health areas were identified because they address leading causes of preventable death and disability; the needed actions are evidence-based, scalable, and feasible; and tools are in place to measure progress. Innovation activities emphasize new approaches to meet specific outcomes in each area, creative ways to communicate with the public using a variety of media platforms; and exploration of new ways that address the know–do gap and foster mainstream adoption. Establishing the concept of communities of practice in which the federal government and partners at the state, territorial, and community level come together to share lessons learned and build and scale successes is critical to making rapid progress.

FOSTERING A CULTURE OF GROWTH AND LEARNING

As we study the work of Thomas Edison, Henry Ford, and other great innovators we quickly realize that much of their success was due to their ability to tap into their knowledge networks and exploit what was already known.[4] When seen this way, innovation becomes less the domain of the lone genius and something within reach of all of us. The following are examples of HHS activities designed to foster a culture of growth and learning.

VISIBLE COMMITMENT BY LEADERSHIP

For many people, innovation is something that is not well understood, unattainable, or perhaps something to be experimented with when routine work is done (which rarely happens). Leaders of organizations can make great strides in setting expectations through very simple means. The CDC Director utilizes all-hands meetings to bring together 15,000 employees that are geographically dispersed across the globe to discuss challenges, accomplishments to date, and specific actions for the path forward. A common theme is the need to improve operational efficiency and a mandate to challenge the status quo by routinely asking three simple questions. "Is this program working? Is this the best we can do? Is there more we can do?" There are important layers of meaning in these words: (1) employees are expected to ask questions; (2) the pursuit of excellence is an expectation of everyone; (3) innovation is about improving efficiency and impact (which are core needs); and (4) innovation is not something you schedule for a percentage of your time but is something you are expected to do all the time. These very simple and clear instructions suddenly make the task of innovation more manageable and behavior easier to change where it matters the most: in the workplace where critical decisions are made on a daily basis.

EMPOWERING INNOVATORS

The lack of systematic processes to help employees transform their ideas into realities is a common barrier of innovation within large organizations. All too often the lack of such processes results in a focus on incremental improvements and extensions of existing work. Worse yet are organizations that seek new ideas but then fail to support their development or implementation. In response to this barrier, the CDC recently launched an intramural competitive program called the Innovation Fund (iFund) and designed it to enable employees to test innovative new ideas that specifically address organizational priorities. The aim of this intramural competition is to help employees with the best ideas develop proof-of-concept data or an early evidence base that will allow the idea to be evaluated for its merit for further development through traditional funding sources. Evaluation has three components: technical review by innovators from across the organization, use of an enterprisewide crowdsourcing platform to provide constructive comments to strengthen impact of proposals, and community voting to select the best ideas that should be funded. The iFund reinforces that employees have innovative ideas, encourages exploration, and demonstrates that ideas are valued by providing the resources needed to make them a reality.

RECOGNIZING INDIVIDUALS FOR INNOVATION

The recognition of individuals for innovation is important for several reasons. Award programs (1) recognize that innovation is not something new to an organization but something that employees already do; (2) establish a standard for excellence in innovation; (3) give tangible examples for what innovation is by allowing employees to see what their peers are doing; (4) create an opportunity to share information and lessons learned about projects developed throughout the organization; and (5) recognize individuals for experimenting, taking on risk, and transforming what was once an idea into something that is valued by others. HHS*innovates* is a department wide recognition program that is led by HHS Secretary Kathleen Sebelius.[11] The program celebrates innovations from across the department in an open nomination process. Candidates are evaluated through a transparent process for creativity and applicability of their programs within HHS or throughout the federal government. The finalists have the opportunity to meet with senior HHS and operational division leaders to present their work and are given awards recognizing their achievements.

CREATING SAFE SPACES FOR EXPERIMENTATION

Learning collaboratives and communities of practice (CoPs) bring together a large number of individuals, organizations, or stakeholders with shared interests to seek improvement in a specific area. Participants may focus on different aspects of the problem of interest and typically share what they are doing, lessons learned, and the latest science from experts. The premise of a learning collaborative creates the mindset of growth and exploration and reduces anxiety for failure. The U.S. Agency for Healthcare Research and Quality (AHRQ) hosts a virtual idea forum called the Health Care Innovations Exchange where participants share and learn about evidence-based innovations and tools that are primarily targeted toward healthcare professionals and researchers.[12] The focus of this program is to accelerate the implementation, adoption, and sustainability of improved methods for delivering quality healthcare. The program allows users to search for innovations within specific topic areas, provides tools for measuring progress, provides multimedia tools and resources to help promote adoption of new practices within organizations, and provides an opportunity to network with others who are working on similar problems. Learning collaboratives set the stage for exploration and create an environment that is accepting of both risk and failure as part of the journey toward improvement.

PROCESSES AND TOOLS THAT FACILITATE INNOVATION

Most innovators working in large organizations encounter common barriers: risk aversion, lack of resources, and the inability to connect with people or information. Processes and tools to develop networked solutions and shared risk models can be helpful in transforming innovative new ideas into a reality. Select examples of HHS programs that facilitate innovation are listed below.

META-LEADERSHIP

Within most organizations there are innovators who independently struggle to test their ideas. Often, they succeed because of their own passion, perseverance, and resourcefulness rather than because of organizational support. Particularly in large global organizations, there is benefit to creating a more coordinated effort to address common barriers, provide overall direction, share best practices, and link related innovation activities across and within the organizations. An example of meta-leadership is the HHS Innovation Council that consists of representatives from staff offices operating divisions. The primary purpose of the council is to create a culture of innovation throughout HHS by cooperatively identifying and removing barriers, cultivating and accelerating the adoption of new technologies, and providing specific points of contact across the department that can support collaborative activities in areas of shared interest.[13]

INNOVATION NETWORKS AND COLLABORATION PLATFORMS

Networks of linked participants demonstrate the power of openly sharing ideas, data, and perspectives from diverse groups of parties that possess highly specialized knowledge. Virtual networks are increasingly being applied to enhance the pace of knowledge sharing and problem solving. Within the biomedical research community, VIVO has an emerging open source network supporting collaboration through a "Facebook-like" environment.[14] VIVO supports browsing and a search function that returns faceted results for rapid retrieval of desired information. Content in any local VIVO installation may be maintained manually, brought into VIVO in automated ways from local systems of record, such as human resources, grants, course and faculty activity databases, or from database providers such as publication aggregators and funding agencies. Similar strategies are unfolding in federally sponsored programs to help promote the integration of electronic health records, promoting the adoption of innovations in healthcare, and alternative health services financing and delivery methods. The "Beacon Communities" program has established a national network of programs designed to share experiences from institutions with advanced adoption with those that are in the early stages of technology adoption.[15] The AHRQ healthcare innovations exchange helps healthcare professionals become aware of and adopt the latest and best methods to provide effective care to patients.[16] As a component of the new legislation being implemented at CMS, a new Center for Innovation has been developing organizational structures with an eye on the future to enable new health delivery models to be created, tested, and evaluated for scalability.[17]

OPEN DATA TO ENHANCE ORGANIZATIONAL PERFORMANCE

Although not often thought of as a key ingredient for innovation, data and data resources are serving as a major new fuel source for re-engineering value-based healthcare models. From encouragement of open data publication of scientific results through the Public Library of Science, to establishing new data resources with automated download features, HHS is promoting data production as a key operational scheme underpinning its Open Government plan, and health reform activities. Not only are surveys and research data being produced this way, but administrative and management data, byproducts of HHS operations, are now being turned into data resources for anyone to use free of charge.

The process involved in translating data into information requires context and understanding of the nature of data and this has opened up a large opportunity for applications developers. Furthermore, the translation of that information to improve quality of performance, and improve efficiency through action is at the core of knowledge management. This last step is admittedly early in its deployment, but here again rest opportunities for competition and innovation. HHS's enterprise activities in healthdata.gov, a common access point for the department's open data resources also provides examples of applications of data aimed at improvements of health in a wide array of applications. Across HHS, other programmatic themes have emerged to improve data liquidity to serve greater public health needs, such as the FDA Sentinel program that uses community level electronic health record information to identify adverse events and support evidence development from uses of medications and devices.[18,19] The cancer Bioinformatics GRID provides open source data and institutes business models to promote its application to guide software development and applications in cancer research.[20] Collectively, organizational efforts support infrastructure that will streamline access to data and information. Providing incentives for creative applications and knowledge management are institutional priorities at HHS to guide decision making across all dimensions of the agency's mission.

CROWDSOURCING

Crowdsourcing is a powerful approach that engages a wide community of problem solvers including entrepreneurs, the public, government, industry, and communities to develop new products or services in order to gain competitive advantage in the market or to solve intransigent problems that benefit society. Challenge and prize competitions are particularly useful for (1) identifying unconventional ideas and exploring the feasibility of their application to specific challenges; (2) engaging traditional and nontraditional communities that include entrepreneurs, the public, and researchers across disciplines to solve scientific, technological, or communication problems; (3) creating awareness of important issues; and (4) sparking innovation in specific areas within and outside of the organization. The America COMPETES Reauthorization Act of 2010 encourages the use of crowdsourcing by the federal government to increase American innovation and global competitiveness through open innovation. HHS and other federal departments and agencies are using challenges and prize formats within and outside their organizations to solve difficult scientific and technical problems and to create awareness of important issues.[21] Examples of challenges include the identification of innovative community programs that promote healthy living; tools to help public health professionals, advocates, and decision makers obtain the data and information they need to design effective public health programs; and applications to promote innovation in health information technologies such as electronic medical record systems.

SUMMARY

There are many motivations for organizations to promote idea generation and risk taking in the workplace: enhanced market share, improved stakeholder value, and overall recognition of leadership in their class of competition. However, the aspirations to be the best are often countered by organizational barriers, culture, and in some cases, fear. Identifying the barriers to innovation often opens the doors for solutions. The qualities that enable openness for exchange of ideas, and fostering free thinking that transcends institutional hierarchy is often challenged and strained from operational rigors and the predictability of systems and processes. Deploying technology platforms and tools to enhance creativity and collaboration can spark teamwork and idea sharing. Creating "safe spaces" and encouraging demonstration projects that allow employees time from their routine responsibilities are often the sparks of innovation leading to addressing some of an organization's most vexing challenges. Promoting special innovation events and employee recognition activities to be publicly viewed can often be the magnet for others to test ideas, challenge dogma, and pursue a higher level of risk than would normally occur. Sharing information and encouraging openness with the public regarding innovation processes are important aspects of managing successful innovation programs, particularly for government.

All organizations stand to risk future productivity and relevance by allowing their management, budget processes, oversight mechanisms, general complacency, and uncertainty to rein in the inspirations and aspirations for employees to problem-solve. These are particularly important factors to consider when in search of new talent or retaining high-performing employees, particularly in highly specialized areas of work. Providing clear examples of risk-taking and the benefits of failure can be important motivators to overcome stagnation. The value systems that all levels of management can establish by organized efforts to promote innovation can be powerful levers of change in taking on increasingly complex challenges, often with diminishing resources.

Government bureaucracies represent unlikely skunkworks for innovation as they are more commonly associated with slowness to change, and are overburdened by process. However, history has shown that opportunities are unique for government, and when recognized and motivated, innovation can have unprecedented results that may not be created in any other space. Using leadership in unconventional ways to promote culture change can and will produce results, often in unpredictable ways.

Disclaimer: The views and opinions of the authors expressed herein do not necessarily state or reflect those of HHS or the United States government.

ENDNOTES

1. Congressional Budget Office (CBO). *The Long-term Budget Outlook*, 2009.
2. Cutler, D. *Where are the Health Care Entrepreneurs? The Failure of Organizational Innovation in Health Care.* Innovation Policy and the Economy, Volume 11, (Josh Lerner and Scott Stern, eds.), Chicago: University of Chicago Press, pp. 1–28. 2010.
3. Rogers, E. *Diffusion of Innovations.* 5th edition, New York: Free Press (Simon & Schuster). 2003.
4. Hargadon, A. *How Breakthroughs Happen:The Surprising Truth About How Companies Innovate.* Boston: Harvard Business School Press. 2003.
5. Haidt, J. *The Happiness Hypothesis: Finding Modern Truth in Ancient Wisdom.* New York: Basic Books. 2006.

6. Heath, C. and Heath, D. *Switch: How to Change Things When Change is Hard.* New York: Broadway Books. 2010.

7. Chesbrough, H. *Open Innovation: The New Imperative for Creating and Profiting from Technology.* Boston: Harvard Business School. 2003.

8. Obama, B. Memorandum for the Heads of Executive Departments and Agencies. *Federal Register*, 74: 15, January 21, 2009.

9. Department of Health and Human Services, *HHS Open Government Plan v1.1 6/25/2010*, http://www.hhs.gov/open/plan/opengovernmentplan/openplanversion1_1.pdf

10. Centers for Disease Control and Prevention, *Winnable Battles*, 04/06/2011 http://www.cdc.gov/WinnableBattles/.

11. Department of Heath and Human Services, *HHSinnovates: Program Overview*, 04/06/2011 http://www.hhs.gov/open/innovate/hhsinnovateoverview.html

12. Department of Health and Human Services, Agency for Healthcare Research and Quality, *AHRQ Health Care Innovations Exchange*, 04/06/2011, http://www.innovations.ahrq.gov/

13. Department of Health and Human Services, *Foster Open Government*, 04/06/2011 http://www.hhs.gov/secretary/about/foster.html

14. VIVO, *An Interdisciplinary National Network*, 04/06/2011, http://vivoweb.org/

15. Maxson E., Jain S., McKethan A., Brammer C., Buntin M., Cronin K., Mostashari F., and Blumenthal, D. Beacon communities aim to use health information technology to transform the delivery of care. *Health Aff.* 2010; 29:1671–1677.

16. Clutter, P. AHRQ Healthcare Exchange: Promoting adoption of innovations. *Crit. Care Nurs. Q.* 2009; 32: 62–68.

17. Guterman, S., Davis, K., Stremikis, K., and Drake, H. Innovation in Medicare and Medicaid will be central to health reform's success. *Health Aff.* 2010; 29: 1188–1193.

18. Platt, R., Wilson M., Chan, K., Benner, J., Marchibroda, J., and McClellan, M. The new sentinel network—Improving the evidence of medical product safety. *N. Engl. J. Med.* 2009; 361: 645–647.

19. Behrman, R., Benner, J., Brown, J., McClellan, M., Woodcock, J., and Platt, R. Developing the Sentinel System – A national resource for evidence development. *N. Engl. J. Med.* 2011;364:498–499.

20. Boyd, L., Hunicke-Smith, S., Staffor, G., Feund, E., Ehlman, M., Chandran, U., Dennis, R., Feranandez, A., Goldstein, S., Steffen, D., Tycko, B., and Klemm, J., *Bioinformatics* Advanced Access online. March 29, 2011.

21. America COMPETES Reauthorization Act of 2010 (H.R. 5116). 111th Congress, 2010.

REFERENCES

Alon, A. (2010). Ten ways to achieve growth through innovation, cio.com, March 10, http://advice.cio.com/charles_hartley/10_ways_to_achieve_growth_through_innovation?page=0%2C0.

Brown, T. (2011). Granting Permission to Innovate, *Harvard Business Review-Agenda 2011*, Cambridge, MA: Harvard Business School Press, January.

Chesbrough, H. (2003). *Open Innovation: The New Imperative for Creating and Profiting from Technology*, Cambridge, MA: Harvard Business School Press.

Jaruzelski, B. and Dehoff, K. (2010). The global innovation 1000: How the top innovators keep winning, *Strategy + Business Magazine*, 61: Winter.

Koetzier, W. and Alon, A. (2009). You need a chief innovation officer, Forbes.com, December 16.

Wall, K. (2010). New report: Booz & Company—Global innovation study, *Innovation Management*, November 4, http://www.innovationmanagement.se/2010/11/04/new-report-booz-company-global-innovation-study/.

Walsh, B. (2010). The electrifying Edison, *Time* magazine, 176: 1, July 5.

Index